Practical Bu

Practical Buddhism

Upāsaka Lu K'uan Yü
(Charles Luk)

RIDER
London Sydney Auckland Johannesburg

Rider & Co Ltd
An imprint of Century Hutchinson Ltd,
Brookmount House, 62-65 Chandos Place, Covent Garden,
London WC2N 4NW

Century Hutchinson Australia (Pty) Ltd
89-91 Albion Street, Surry Hills, New South Wales 2010, Australia

Century Hutchinson New Zealand Limited
PO Box 40-086, 32-34 View Road, Glenfield, Auckland 10, New Zealand

Century Hutchinson South Africa (Pty) Limited
PO Box 337, Bergvlei 2012, South Africa

First published in Great Britain 1971
This edition 1988

Set in Bembo type

Printed and bound in Great Britain by
Anchor Brendon Ltd, Tiptree, Essex

British Cataloguing in Publication Data

Lu K'uan Yü, *1898–1979*
    Practical Buddhism.
    1. Buddhism
    I. Title
    294.3

ISBN 0 7126 1735 3

Contents

Preface   ix

PART I   The Buddha-Dharma (Theory and Practice)   1

PART II The Story of the Third Ch'an Patriarch of China
         and his gāthā 'Have Faith In Your Mind' (Hsin Hsin
         Ming)   33

PART III The Ch'an Shout, by Ch'an Master Chi Ch'eng   39

PART IV Master Han Shan's Experiment with the Mind   43

PART V   The Autobiography of Ch'an Master Han Shan   57

         Glossary   163

To the memory of
Upāsikā Grace Constant Lounsbery
Founder and President of 'Les Amis du Bouddhisme'
whose words of encouragement overcame the author's
hesitation when he began to translate Chinese texts
in 1956

Preface

We take refuge in the Buddha,
We take refuge in the Dharma,
We take refuge in the Saṅgha,
We take refuge in the Triple Gem within ourselves.

After the publication of our five books, the three series of *Ch'an and Zen Teaching*, *The Secrets of Chinese Meditation* and *The Śūraṅgama Sūtra*, we have found it useful to present this book so that readers will have more information on the Buddha Dharma and its practice. This volume contains five parts:

Part I outlines the theory and practice of the Buddha's doctrine which is divided into the teaching school and the transmission of mind outside the teaching.

The teaching school comprises Hīnayāna or preparatory instruction, and Mahāyāna or advanced and final courses.

Hīnayāna is based on the three signata or seals of impermanence of all phenomena, the absence of an ego and peace in Nirvāṇa or the state of extinction of passion and suffering.

In this section we present various methods of meditation in conformity with the four noble truths, the twelve links in the chain of existence and the eightfold correct path which are the tenets of Hīnayāna to put an end to suffering in order to reach relative Nirvāṇa.

Mahāyāna which is much more profound teaches the six perfections or pāramitās which are necessary for Bodhisattva development into Buddhahood. It teaches the wiping out of all dualities, relativities and contraries to leap to the absolute state of the uncreate.

In this section we present various methods of Mahāyāna practice.

The transmission of mind outside of the teaching points direct to

the mind for the perception of Buddha-nature and attainment of
Buddhahood.

This section deals with various techniques such as the kung ans and
the hua t'ou with the feeling of doubt.

In order to acquaint readers with the transmission of mind we
present two cases of spiritual awakening (Chinese, wu, and Japanese,
satori) achieved by two modern Buddhists, a European and an
Englishman, in spite of the scepticism of a reviewer of my first three
books who claims that the Dharma is not suitable for Westerners.
It seems that the European Buddhist achieved the Tathāgata's ch'an
and the English Buddhist the Patriarch's ch'an. (For these two terms
cf *Ch'an and Zen Teaching, First Series,* page 130. Rider, London.)

Part II tells a short story of the third Ch'an patriarch Seng Ts'an
and his well-known gāthā Hsin Hsin Ming (Have faith in your mind)
which teaches how to realise the mind in order to achieve enlightenment.

This section is most important for students of the Mind Dharma
for it not only tells how the third patriarch achieved Enlightenment
(Bodhi) but also how to meditate on the mind for this purpose.

In *Part III* we present a form of kung an (koan) which consists of
giving shouts as demonstrated by Ch'an master Chi Ch'eng who
defeated a Dharma master regarded as a skilful interpreter of the
Hua Yen (Avataṁsaka) School.

This section is most important for students of both the teaching
school and the transmission of mind outside the teaching.

Part IV outlines the training and realisation of bodhi by master
Han Shan of the Ming dynasty so that readers can compare it with
the achievements of the two contemporary European Buddhists
mentioned in Part I of this volume.

Part V contains the said master Han Shan's autobiography which
is most interesting and fascinating in that it gives a full account of his
childhood, his early and advanced training and his final realisation
of Enlightenment. Thus readers will have a clear picture of how
bodhi can be attained in a lifetime.

UPĀSAKA LU K'UAN YÜ

Hong Kong

PART I

The Buddha-Dharma
(Theory and Practice)

THE Sanskrit word *Buddha* means *The Enlightened One*, that is one who understands the chain of causality which leads to worldly existence and suffering, and who succeeds in realising the unreality of the latter, thereby wiping out ignorance and all its consequences, and achieving absolute freedom and comfortable independence.

Twenty-five centuries ago a young prince of the Śākya clan in north India, named Gautama Siddhārtha, left his home in search of the Truth, disciplined himself, and, in his thirty-fifth year, realised Enlightenment after gazing at the stars in the sky. After being released from the illusion of birth and death, this holy man, who became Śākyamuni Buddha, exclaimed: 'It is wonderful that all living beings possess the Tathāgata's wisdom which they are unable to experience solely because of their false thinking and clinging.'

For over forty years Śākyamuni Buddha taught His disciples how to extricate themselves from worldly entanglements in order to realise Enlightenment (Bodhi). This is what we call *The Teaching School*. But the absolute state of Bodhi is beyond all relativities and contraries, and cannot be expressed in human conditioned language. Therefore, one day in the assembly the Buddha held up a flower, a gesture which His chief disciple Mahākāśyapa alone understood and acknowledged with a smile. Thereat the Buddha declared to him: 'I have the treasure of the right Dharma Eye, Nirvāna's wonderful mind and the immaterial Reality which I now transmit to you.'

This is *The Transmission outside of the Teaching* which is called Ch'an (Japanese, Zen).

I. THE TEACHING SCHOOL

According to the T'ien T'ai (Japanese, Tendai) School, the Buddha's teaching was in five stages. In the first stage of three weeks, He explained *The Avataṁsaka Sūtra* which only Bodhisattvas understood, as it was beyond the comprehension of His disciples. In the second stage of twelve years, He taught *The Āgamas*, urging His followers to forsake their attachments to the concepts of ego and phenomena (dharma) in order to rest temporarily in the Hīnayāna's relative Nirvāṇa. After they had made further progress, He taught them the Hīnayāna-cum-Mahāyāna or *Vaipulya* doctrines in the third stage of eight years to help them develop the Mahāyāna mind. After they had been initiated into Mahāyāna, He taught them the *Prajñā Sūtras* in the fourth stage of twenty-two years to arouse their inherent wisdom so that it could manifest and function normally. In the fifth stage of eight years, He taught the *Lotus Sūtra* to open their minds to the One Buddha Vehicle which transcends the three expedient vehicles of Śrāvakas, Pratyeka-buddhas and Bodhisattvas, by *revealing* it to them so that they could *awaken* to and *enter* it. Therefore, the aim of His teaching did not go beyond the four words: opening, revealing, awakening and entering.[1] Before passing away, in a day and night, He taught them *The Mahāparinirvāṇa Sūtra* to reveal the four absolute realities of *Eternity, Bliss, Self*[2] and *Purity* in the Ultimate Nirvāṇa.

So we know that at the beginning of His teaching the Buddha did not reveal the whole Truth which was beyond the comprehension of His disciples. Hence his gradual exposition of it, and, though the same words and terms were used throughout the five periods of teaching, they had deeper meanings in each more advanced stage.

[1] Cf *Ch'an and Zen Teaching, Third Series, The Altar Sūtra of the Sixth Patriarch*, p. 61. Rider, London.
[2] Self is omnipresent and omniscient entity as contrasted with Ego which is limited to sense organs and sense data.

The import of the rules of discipline, of the Four Noble Truths, of
the Eightfold Path and of the Twelve links in the chain of existence
was partially explained to Hīnayāna disciples and fully revealed to
them only after they had developed the Mahāyāna mind. The
precepts taught to Śrāvakas were not as all-embracing as those to be
observed by Bodhisattvas. For instance, the five prohibitions for
beginners against killing, stealing, carnality, intoxicating drink and
lying were broadened to include the mere thought and desire of
committing these evils. And only after His disciples had well understood the three vehicles of Śrāvaka, Pratyeka-buddha and Bodhisattva did the Buddha disclose in *The Lotus Sūtra* that these were only
expedients taught to disciples of low, medium and high spirituality
so that they could disengage themselves first from *coarse* concepts
and then from *subtle* views of the reality of ego and things, for the
sole purpose of awakening them to the Buddha Vehicle which was
the real aim of His teaching. Finally He revealed in *The Mahāparinirvāṇa Sūtra* the real meanings of all the words and terms that He
had used for over forty years. This gradual revelation of the Truth
was referred to by Ch'an master Lin Chi (Japanese, Rinzai) as
temporal and real teaching.[1]

Therefore, it is of paramount importance for sincere seekers of
the Dharma to study first the Hīnayāna and then the Mahāyāna
before they can realise that the Buddha was at great pains to guide
and lead His disciples, as well as ourselves in this Dharma ending
age, out of the realm of illusion and suffering. In our study and
practice of His Dharma, we should begin by burying pride and
prejudice to cultivate the two great Buddhist virtues which are
modesty and humility, and by keeping the commandment to live
purely in order to avoid disturbing our minds. It is only after we
have understood the doctrine of suffering, unreality, impermanence
and absence of ego as taught by the Buddha to Hīnayāna disciples,
and so have created a congenial atmosphere for advanced training that
we can make further progress and thereby correctly interpret the
Mahāyāna which is beyond the reach of the discriminating mind.

We should be sincere in our study and practice of the Dharma so

[1] Cf *Ch'an and Zen Teaching, Second Series,* pp. 95–6. Rider, London.

that we can advance on the right Path which, however, can be easily blocked by the personality cult and the search for fame and money which are incompatible with the holy teaching. In *The Śūraṅgama Sūtra*[1] the Buddha says that Tathāgata-mongers will be found everywhere to distort the holy teaching in the Dharma ending age. Many Westerners are weary of materialism and are keen to seek the Truth but unfortunately they are handicapped by the paucity of authentic versions of Mahāyāna and Ch'an texts and by the absence of men of good counsel (kalyāṇamitra) who are competent to teach the right Dharma.

(A) THE HĪNAYĀNA TEACHING

The Hīnayāna teaching is based on Three Signata or Seals of impermanence, absence of an ego and peace in Nirvāṇa. Because of our dislike of suffering and impermanence in the three realms of desire, of form and beyond form, we awaken to the non-existence of an ego and seek permanence in Nirvāṇa. The Four Noble Truths are the foundation teaching for Śrāvakas (hearers) and the Twelve Nidānas or links in the chain of existence are that for Pratyeka-buddhas who seek self-enlightenment.

The Four Noble Truths
Since we know that our transmigration through the three realms of existence is caused by karma, we seek to avoid being involved in the law of causality by studying the Four Noble Truths, which are: *suffering* which is an attribute of mortal life; *accumulation* of karmic causes which leads to continued suffering; *extinction* of suffering and the *Path* thereto. The correct Path leading to extinction of suffering is eightfold and comprises:
    Correct view,
    Correct thought,
    Correct speech,
    Correct conduct,
    Correct livelihood,

[1] Cf my translation of *The Śūraṅgama Sūtra*. Rider, London, 1965.

Correct devotion,
Correct mindfulness, and
Correct meditation.

Therefore, the Three Dharma-seals and Four Noble Truths are interrelated as follows:

The Three Dharma-seals: *The Four Noble Truths:*

Impermanence ———————— Suffering
Absence of ego ————————— Accumulation
Nirvāna ———————————— Extinction
                            Path

As to the method of practice, such as the fivefold, fourfold and sixteenfold meditations, they are based on the Four Noble Truths as follows:

The Fivefold Meditation:
on counting the breath ——————— Suffering
on impurity ————
on compassion————— Accumulation
on causality ————
on separateness (the six sense ———— Path
organs, their objects and perceptions)

The Fourfold Meditation:
on body as being impure and filthy ——— Suffering
on sensation as resulting in suffering ——
on mind as being impermanent ———— Accumulation
on dharma as without independent nature ——→ Path

The Sixteenfold Meditation:

Suffering		
	Suffering	meditation on the body which is subject to suffering.
	Voidness	meditation on causal creations which are unreal.
	Impermanence	meditation on causal creations which are impermanent.
	Absence of ego	meditation on causal creations which are devoid of ego.

Accumulation	Accumulation	meditation on the accumulation of karmic suffering.
	Cause	meditation on the cause of suffering.
	Stay	meditation on continued suffering.
	Circumstance	meditation on circumstances leading to suffering.
Extinction	Extinction	meditation on the end of the worldly stream leading to the extinction of birth and death.
	Stillness	meditation on the eradication of the three poisons leading to stillness of mind.
	Comfort	meditation on the way out of the three realms of existence leading to an end of all troubles.
	Freedom	meditation on the eradication of all troubles.
Path	Path	meditation on the Path that leads to Nirvāṇa.
	Reality	the Path accords with the correct doctrine and ensures the attainment of Nirvāṇa.
	Practice	practice and treading the Path that leads to Nirvāṇa.
	Way out	the Path that leads to the way out of Saṁsāra.

The four stages in Hīnayāna attainment are: śrota-āpanna (entering the holy stream), sakṛdāgāmin (once more to come or be reborn in the world of desire), anāgāmin (no coming or no more rebirth), and Arhatship (beyond the worldly way).

The Twelve Nidānas
Pratyeka-buddhas are those who live apart from others and attain enlightenment alone or for themselves, in contrast with the Bodhi-

sattva altruism. They awaken to the Twelve links in the chain of existence which are:

Past life	1. Ignorance	Unenlightenment due to past passions.
	2. Disposition	Past karmic disposition leading to present incarnation.
Present life	3. Consciousness	Present incarnation in foetus.
	4. Name and Form	Gradual development of foetus.
	5. The six sense organs	Formation of sense organs, ready for birth.
	6. Touch	Childhood in which intelligence is limited to impressions.
	7. Sensation	Development of feelings of like and dislike.
	8. Desire	Desire and craving for sense data.
	9. Grasping	The urge of sensuous existence.
	10. Becoming	Formation of present karma leading to the next incarnation.
Future life	11. Rebirth	Consciousness in the present life causing rebirth in the next life.
	12. Old age and death	Name and form, sense organs, touch and sensation in the present life leading to old age, illness and death in the next reincarnation.

The classical formula of the Twelve Nidānas reads: from ignorance, disposition; from disposition, consciousness; from consciousness, name and form; from name and form, the six sense organs; from the six sense organs, contact; from contact, sensation; from sensation, desire; from desire, grasping; from grasping, becoming; from becoming, birth; from birth, old age and death.

These Twelve Nidānas are identical with the first two Noble Truths, suffering and accumulation, and their endings are identical with the last two Noble Truths, extinction and the Path thereto. These are the whole method of contemplation by Pratyeka-buddhas.

(B) THE MAHĀYĀNA TEACHING

As said earlier, Hīnayāna is based on the Three Signata or Three Dharma-seals of *impermanence, egolessness* and *peace in Nirvāṇa* which should be the subject of our study at the start, to be followed up with the Mahāyāna teaching of Six Pāramitās, or perfections in almsgiving (dāna), morality (śīla), forbearance (kṣānti), devotion (vīrya), meditation (dhyāna) and wisdom (prajñā) which are necessary for the realisation of the *One Reality* of the Buddha vehicle, the basis on Dharma-seal of Mahāyāna as revealed in *The Lotus Sūtra*.

The Four Noble Truths and the Twelve Nidānas studied by Śrāvakas and Pratyeka-buddhas during the Hīnayāna period of teaching will be found by them to have much deeper meanings when they develop the Mahāyāna mind. They will realise that suffering, accumulation, extinction and the Path thereto as well as the Twelve Links in the Chain of Existence are but illusions which have no room in the absolute state wherein all relativities and contraries cease to exist as taught in *The Heart Sūtra*.[1]

When the Buddha teaches the Four Noble Truths and the Twelve Nidānas—in fact the same Dharma, some listeners awaken to suffering, impermanence, egolessness and peace in Nirvāṇa whereas others develop the Mahāyāna mind, wipe out all dualities and leap over both the mundane and supramundane to reach the absolute state of Bhūtatathatā. Therefore, the same words spoken by the Buddha are differently interpreted by men of low, medium and high spirituality. Hence Lin Chi says: 'He who hits the first rate meaning is fit to teach Patriarchs and Buddhas; he who hits the second rate meaning

[1] Cf *Ch'an and Zen Teaching, First Series, Part IV, The Heart Sūtra.* Rider, London.

is fit to teach men and devas; and he who hits the third rate meaning
is even unfit to save himself.'[1]

Therefore, Hīnayāna sūtras can be readily understood at first
reading but Mahāyāna scriptures are very profound, and serious
students should first cast away pride, prejudice and preconceived
ideas, and then read the texts as many times as required in order to
discover newer and deeper meanings at each re-reading until, after
forgetting all about expedient terms and idioms, they comprehend
the teaching and embody it in their deeds, words and thoughts; the
impact of such embodiment is terrific and changes them completely.
They will feel as if the words spoken by the Buddha to His disciples
were meant for themselves, with His voice clearly audible after each
re-reading. They will realise their errors and mistakes since time
without beginning, and will shed tears of remorse. This is the
moment when their excellent roots or inner qualities, hitherto
dormant, manifest as described by master Chih I, the Fourth
Patriarch of the T'ien T'ai School.[2] Henceforth nothing on earth
can deter their quest of Enlightenment.

The Unreality of Worldly Existence

The Buddha says in *The Śūraṅgama Sūtra*: 'Virtuous men, I have
always declared that form and mind and all causes arising there-
from, all mental conditions and all causal phenomena are but
manifestations of the mind. Your bodies and minds are just appear-
ances within the wonderful, bright and pure Profound Mind. Why
do you stray from the precious, bright and subtle nature of fundamentally Enlightened Mind and so recognise delusion within
Enlightenment?

'Mind's Dimness creates dull Emptiness and both, in the darkness,
unite with it to become Form. The mingling of Form with false
thinking causes the latter to take the shape of a body. Stirred by
accumulated causes within and drawn to externals without, such
inner disturbance is mistaken for the nature of mind, hence the false

---

[1] Cf *Ch'an and Zen Teaching, Second Series*, p. 93. Rider, London.
[2] Cf *The Secrets of Chinese Meditation, The T'ien T'ai School*, p. 140. Rider,
London.

view of a mind dwelling in the physical body and the failure to realise that this body as well as external mountains, rivers, space and the great earth are but phenomena within the wondrous bright True Mind. Like an ignorant man who overlooks the great ocean but grasps at a floating bubble and regards it as the whole body of water in its immense expanse, you are doubly deluded amongst the deluded.'

Therefore, all things including man's body and mind as well as the universe are created by his ālaya-vijñāna which is the store of consciousness whose three characteristics are: *self-evidencing, perception* and *form. Self-evidencing* is ālaya's awareness of itself; *perception* is its function of perceiving phenomena; and *form* comprises all things so perceived, which include body, mind and the world. Thus from nothingness spring self, others and the world which are fundamentally unreal and continue to exist in the realm of illusions.

The Teaching consists in wiping out *form* which comprises all things that are unreal and depend on discrimination for their seeming existence. When *perception* confronts no more objects, it vanishes of itself and exposes *self-evidencing* ālaya which is likened to a second moon seen by weak eyes. When this second moon is cognised as a reflection of the real moon, it will disappear and expose the latter, or the One Mind which will lead to the perception of self-nature and attainment of Buddhahood. This is fully explained in *The Śūraṅgama Sūtra*.

The Mahāyāna Mind

As the Buddha says in *The Diamond Sūtra*,[1] He has no fixed Dharma to teach to others for His consists in wiping out all their false thoughts and discriminations, one by one, until these are completely rooted out so that the inherent wisdom in all men is no more screened by ignorance and can function as it should.

Therefore, in the stage of Hīnayāna teaching, the Buddha wipes out all *coarse conceptions* of ego and dharma (things) by expounding the Four Noble Truths and the Twelve Nidānas to beginners who

[1] Cf *Ch'an and Zen Teaching, First Series, The Diamond Cutter of Doubts*. Rider, London.

can only digest this incomplete truth. After they have awakened to the Hīnayāna doctrines, He reveals to them that there still exist in them *subtle views* of self and dharma which are so subtle that they are imperceptible and which should be wiped out as well to develop the Mahāyāna mind.

Methods of Mahāyāna Practice

Viewed from their underlying nature (Dharmatā), all things that spring from it are identical with Reality, and all living beings are essentially Buddhas, being free from troubles (kleśa) and being fundamentally enlightened; hence there is no kleśa to wipe out, no Dharma to practise and no Bodhi to realise. But viewed from the realm of phenomena it can be asked: Who is free from troubles and who can become Buddha by merely stating that he is fundamentally enlightened? So before living beings awaken to Reality and are liberated, the Buddha teaches boundless expedient methods so that they can practise them to wipe out delusion and achieve liberation. And since there are men of slow and quick propensities, the Buddha teaches the corresponding gradual and quick methods to guide them out of the realm of illusion.

The gradual method comprises fifty-six stages of Bodhisattva development into Buddhahood: the ten stages each of Bodhisattva faith and wisdom, the ten lines of Bodhisattva action, the ten acts of Bodhisattva dedication, the four additional harnessing stages, the ten Bodhisattva positions, the stage of Universal Enlightenment (substance) and that of Wonderful Enlightenment (function), which require three asaṅkhyeyas or innumerable aeons to achieve, the first to hear about the Dharma, the second to practise it and the third to realise it. This is fully explained in *The Śūraṅgama Sūtra*.

As to the sudden method, all living beings possess the Buddha-nature which is screened by ignorance since time without beginning, hence their drifting about in the sea of saṁsāra; if this veil of delusion is destroyed, their Buddha-nature will manifest instantaneously, and there is no need to pass through the above fifty-six stages. Hence the realisation of Enlightenment in the time of a thought. This is what the various sudden schools mean by *body is Buddha*, *mind is Buddha* and *perception of self-nature and attainment of Buddhahood,* without setting up any gradual stages of achievement. Both the gradual and sudden schools do not go beyond the realisation of the One Reality of the Buddha vehicle.

The Avalokiteśvara Method

There are many methods of Mahāyāna practice and we have presented a few important ones in *The Secrets of Chinese Meditation.* According to *The Śūraṅgama Sūtra,* the most suitable method for human beings is that practised by Avalokiteśvara Bodhisattva. It consists in directing the organ of hearing into the stream of meditation to disengage it from its object, and then to wipe out the concept of both sound and stream-entry until both disturbance and stillness cease to exist. In time both hearing and its object will come to an end, resulting in a state of purity and cleanness which should not be clung to. When the awareness of this state and this state itself are realised as non-existent, both subject and object merge into the void, the awareness of which becomes all-embracing. With further elimination of the void and its opposite, both creation and annihilation vanish, giving way to the state of Nirvāṇa which manifests and ensures a leap over both the mundane and supramundane. This is how Avalokiteśvara Bodhisattva realised Enlightenment.

Readers will find in Han Shan's Autobiography presented in Part V of this volume that the famous master successfully practised the same Avalokiteśvara method which consists in directing the organ of hearing into the stream of meditation in order to disengage himself from sound and so realise Enlightenment.

The Prajñā-pāramitā Method

Another method, called the Prajñā-pāramitā, which was strongly recommended by the Fifth and Sixth Ch'an Patriarchs, and which was followed by eminent masters in China, consists in reading only *The Diamond Sūtra* and in picking out a single sentence or gāthā which the devotee memorises in order to look into its profound meaning, and apply it to his daily activities which involve deed, word and thought, so that he will not stray from the Teaching. And so, by picking out, one by one, all the other sentences and gāthās of the sūtra and embodying their profound meanings in all common acts of daily life, he will in time identify himself with the whole Dharma and thereby develop a mind that *does not abide anywhere* and becomes all-embracing. Thus disengaged from sense organs, their objects and their perceptions, he will achieve prajñā-pāramitā and the patient endurance of the Uncreate which will lead to Enlightenment.

The recitation of *The Diamond Sūtra* is always followed by that of *The Heart Sūtra* which, after wiping out the worldly man's attachment to the five aggregates, the Śrāvaka's clinging to the Four Noble Truths, the Pratyeka-buddha's concept of the Twelve Nidānas and the Bodhisattva's notion of Bodhi and Realisation, teaches the Heart mantra:

Gate, gate, pāragate, pārasaṃgate, Bodhi, svāhā!

which means: 'O Bodhi which has gone, gone, gone to the other shore, gone beyond the other shore—thus fulfilled!' and on which the devotee should always concentrate pointedly to cut down all coarse and subtle concepts of subjective ego and objective Dharma, in order to attain the absolute state free from the duality of *this shore of delusion* and *the other shore of Enlightenment* so that he can leap over both the mundane and supramundane as taught by Avalokiteśvara Bodhisattva.

This Prajñā-pāramitā method can be practised only by men of the highest spirituality and is beyond the reach of those who are incapable of forsaking worldly pursuits and attachments. We are glad that two learned readers of ours, one in Europe and one in America, have discovered this proper way of reciting *The Diamond and Heart Sūtras*, and have thus dispelled the popular wrong belief that only superstitious people recite sūtras.

The Pure Land Method

The most popular method of the Pure Land School consists of constantly calling the name of Amitābha Buddha who, when he was Bhikṣu Dharmākara in a former life, took the profound vow of liberating all living beings who believe in the law of causality, practise the three formulas of refuge (in Buddha, Dharma and Saṅgha), keep the five precepts, live purely by giving up all worldly attachments, and implore his aid in their quest of Bodhi in his Western Paradise of Bliss.

In practice, the devotee uses a rosary of 108 beads to repeat Amitābha's name, noting down on a sheet of paper the number of daily repetitions which should gradually increase until he achieves stillness of mind. This rosary of 108 beads enables him to call that Buddha 108 times to wipe out 108 karmic bonds for attainment of Buddhahood, to invoke the 108 Holy Ones in the Vajradhātu to protect the repeater, to arouse the 54 characteristics of his potential so that he can achieve the 54 stages of Bodhisattva development into Buddhahood, and to realise 108 kinds of Samādhi; it has the same meaning as the 108 tolls of the monastery bell at dawn and dusk.

The devotee should make pointed concentration on Amitābha Buddha while calling his name either with or without a rosary, as many times as he can until he is disengaged from seeing, hearing, feeling and knowing, thereby realising the pure and clean mind. At the same time, he should cultivate compassion for all living beings and take a great vow similar to that of Bhikṣu Dharmākara. When his vow and that of Amitābha mingle and unite, the combined force will be irresistible and will sweep away all obstructions to the integration of the devotee's pure and clean mind into the Bodhi-mind of the Buddha of Infinite Light. This is the most wonderful method of seeking rebirth in the Western Paradise of Bliss where the devotee will receive instruction direct from Amitābha and his two assistant Bodhisattvas, and will tread the holy path without hindrance.

When they find it difficult to wipe out their thoughts, most ch'an monks in China repeat Amitābha Buddha's name to still their minds before beginning their practice of the kung an or hua t'ou technique. After their ch'an meditation, and especially when they go out, they repeat that Buddha's name to keep away from disturb-ances in order to be on the alert under all circumstances. As to advanced disciples who have succeeded in giving rise to the i-ch'ing or feeling of doubt, they always hold on to it day and night as described in the following chapter on ch'an training.

When I was young I met many foreigners in China who regarded this repetition of Amitābha's name to be a superstitious practice, but according to my personal experience it contributed most effectively to still my mind, and I found nothing wrong in this method which is quite profitable. When the mind is disengaged from externals, the repeater will experience the same manifestation of radiant serenity within and without his own body and the same weightlessness and comfort felt by a practiser of Ch'an who has made substantial progress in his training. Therefore, only those who cannot forsake worldly pursuits in the realm of illusion are really superstitious and pitiable.

The T'ien T'ai Method
The T'ien T'ai teaching, which we have presented in *The Secrets of Chinese Meditation* (Rider, London), can be condensed into two words, chih and kuan. Chih is silencing the active mind to stop all thinking and discrimination, and kuan is looking into the mind thus stripped of them for the purpose of restoring our inherent Buddha-nature.

Practice of chih kuan is to regulate the body and mind so as to stop all rising thoughts, and then to develop an insight into the still mind which becomes pure and clean, and causes wisdom to manifest. However, it is not easy to adjust chih and kuan to each other so that dhyāna and prajñā can be in equilibrium, that is in the condition of the 'mean'. Therefore, the T'ien T'ai school formulates the three-fold meditative study of *k'ung* or noumenon which is void and immaterial; *chia* or phenomenon which is material; and *chung* or the mean from which both noumenon and phenomenon spring.

2. CH'AN OR MIND TRANSMISSION OUTSIDE OF TEACHING

The Teaching cannot reveal the Absolute, for human language is conditioned by worldly relativities and contraries, and can never reach the inconceivable and the inexpressible. There is, however, inherent in man a potentiality which no amount of teaching can reach and which, if properly aroused by Ch'an practice, can come into contact with Reality and unite with it.

Ch'an practice will succeed only if the student observes the rules of discipline (śīla) to quiet his mind and achieve stillness (dhyāna) which causes his inherent wisdom (prajñā) to manifest. The three-fold study of śīla, dhyāna and prajñā is likened to a tripod which supports the Mind Dharma and can stand only if all its three legs are sound.

Although Ch'an surpasses all other methods of practice, the student cannot dispense with the Buddha's teachings in the sūtras because in the absence of enlightened masters in this Dharma ending age he must rely on the Scriptures to adjust and improve the various stages of meditation and so avoid the fifty mental states caused by the five aggregates as described in *The Śūraṅgama Sūtra*.

Instead of passing through all the stages of Bodhisattva develop-ment into Buddhahood as described in the Teaching school, the Ch'an method, which is a shortcut to Enlightenment, begins with the quest of mind as the point of departure; it consists in wiping out all thoughts that stir the mind to prevent it from wandering outside in search of sense data which alone preserve the seeming existence of birth and death. When the mind is no more disturbed by thoughts it will manifest in its all-embracing state. This is precisely what the Sixth Patriarch meant when he said to Hui Ming: 'Do not think of either good or evil, at the very moment when there is no thought in your mind, what is the Venerable Hui Ming's fundamental face?'[1] This is also what the Buddha meant when He said in *The Sūtra of Complete Enlightenment*: 'When one keeps from illusions, one is enlightened without passing through any gradual stages'[2] for illusions are created by thoughts, and when thoughts cease and illusions vanish, the Bodhi mind appears. This is also what Lin Chi

[1] Cf *Ch'an and Zen Teaching, Third Series, The Altar Sūtra*, p. 27. Rider, London.
[2] Cf *Ch'an and Zen Teaching, Third Series, The Sūtra of Complete Enlightenment*, p. 181. Rider, London.

meant when he said: 'If you have no faith in your Self (i.e. self-mind) you will be flustered and will cling to externals which will replace your Self and you will lose your freedom. If you can only stop every thought in your searching mind, you will not differ from the Patriarchs and the Buddhas.'[1]

(A) DIRECT POINTING AT THE MIND

In ancient times people lived very simply and had few desires which they could easily forsake when they were taught to do so in order to look into their minds. This is why when Ma Tsu said: 'Mind is Buddha', his pupil Hui Hai succeeded in realising his self-mind and thereby became enlightened.[2]

This is too simple to be believed, but a serious student wishing to know why Hui Hai awakened should be familiar with the profound meanings of the two idioms *Host* and *Guest* which were so frequently used by Ch'an masters when teaching their disciples, and which derived from *The Śūraṅgama Sūtra* in which Ājñāta-Kauṇḍinya declared to the Buddha:

'I am now a senior in the assembly in which I am the only one who has acquired the art of interpreting because of my awakening to the two words *foreign dust* which led to my attainment of the holy fruit.

'World Honoured One, foreign dust is like a *guest* who stops at at an inn where he passes the night or takes his meal, and as soon as he has done so, he packs and continues his journey because he has no time to stay longer. As to the *host* of the inn, he has nowhere to go. My deduction is that one who does not stay is a *guest* and one who does stay is a *host*. Consequently a thing is foreign when it does not stay.

'Again, in a clear sky when the sun rises and its light enters the house through an opening, the dust is seen moving in the ray of light whereas the empty space is unmoving. Therefore, that which is still is the void and that which moves is the dust.'

[1] Cf *Ch'an and Zen Teaching, Second Series*, p. 112. Rider, London.
[2] Cf John Blofeld's *The Zen Teaching of Hui Hai*. Rider, London.

Consequently *Host* stands for the unchanging self-nature which
is real and *Guest* for phenomena which change continuously and are
unreal. Hui Hai achieved Bodhi because he did not stray from the
Host while keeping away from the *Guest*. When he identified himself with Reality, unreality disappeared; hence his Enlightenment.

In order to acquaint readers with the doctrine of mind, we
present in Part II of this volume a translation of the *Story of the Third
Patriarch Seng Ts'an* with his well-known gāthā 'Have Faith in Your
Mind' (Hsin Hsin Ming).

(B) THE KUNG AN TECHNIQUE

With the advance of material civilisation which lowered man's
spirituality, the great masters were compelled to devise the Kung An
(Japanese, Koan) technique to strip the student of seeing, hearing,
feeling and knowing so that his mind could be set at rest and he
could attain the state of dhyāna which causes prajñā to manifest.

There are many Kung Ans which can be found in the books, but
the one which was very popular in China before and is now used by
most Japanese roshis (Zen teachers) is: 'A monk asked Chao Chou,
"Does a dog have the Buddha-nature?" Chao Chou replied, "No."'
In this Kung An stress is on the word NO which the master urges his
pupil to look into and which the latter believes is the key to success.
So day and night he concentrates his mind on this NO. If he thinks,
'The Buddha says that all living beings including dogs have their
Buddha-nature . . .' even before he tries to argue with Chao Chou,
he knocks against the categorical NO which already looms before
him. If he tries to accept Chao Chou's interpretation which is
definitely contrary to the Buddha's teaching, as soon as he wants to
argue one way or the other, he again knocks against this uncon-
ditional NO. So in whatever direction he may turn to solve this
seemingly insoluble Kung An, he knocks his head against this
implacable NO which blocks every exit and does not allow his mind
to go any further. Thus he finds himself as if imprisoned in a
circular wall made of a countless number of NOs which close in to
isolate his monkey mind and to disengage it from externals to his

great discomfort which may last for months and years during which the force of habits contracted since time without beginning gradually diminishes, causing him to look dull, stupid and haggard. For his monkey mind is turned upside down, he does not see anything in front of him, he hears only the sound of the word NO, his breath seems to be choked and he is even mindless of eating and drinking. This is the moment the Kung An takes effect. His wandering mind, which was sharp and agile before, is now like a wild beast which is trapped and completely exhausted after long efforts to gain freedom. When the monkey mind has exhausted its ingenuity while playing with the word NO, it gradually weakens and becomes impotent; this is precisely the first aim of the training, and the enlightened master notices with satisfaction the result achieved by his pupil. This exhausted mind is likened to a stone girl about to move in a dance and a wooden man ready to sing his song, for the death of the wandering mind is automatically followed by the resurrection of the pure and clean mind, which enables the student to see clearly that the aim of the Kung An is the search for neither dog nor Buddha-nature nor the negative NO. Free from discriminating and discerning caused by the three empty words, his mind transcends the notions of yes and no, *is* and *is not*, and dog and Buddha-nature, perceives beyond all relativities and contraries and attains to the absolute state which is inconceivable and inexpressible, and which only he can appreciate like a drinker of water who alone knows whether it is cold or warm. This state cannot be explained to worldlings but can be communicated only to a few experienced men who have followed the same Path. Hence Lin Chi said:

'When you meet a fencing master, show to him your sword.
Do not give your poem to a man who is not a poet.'[1]

If the student fails in his practice after long and continuous training with this Kung An, this shows that either he misinterprets it or that it does not suit his nature. In the first case he should ponder over his failure which is invariably caused by his clinging to the three

[1] Cf *Ch'an and Zen Teaching, Second Series, The Lin Chi Sect,* p. 106. Rider, London.

empty words (dog, Buddha-nature and No) which are all foreign
dust by taking the *guest* stand. If he finds out his mistake, he should
immediately take up the *host* position to keep from all discriminating
and discerning. If he so adjusts his meditation he will suddenly
achieve the aim of his training.

In the second case, the Kung An may be out of tune with the
nature of the student; he should try another one to avoid wasting
his precious time. There are many Kung Ans in the books in which
he can find one to his liking. Cases are known of monks who
realised the Mind Dharma after changing their Kung Ans.

When a student achieves the unperturbed state of dhyāna, he will
suddenly feel as if he is rid of a heavy burden that has always
weighed on him since time without beginning, and will experience
the weightlessness which astronauts feel while flying in space. At the
same time his body, mind and surroundings, all worldly troubles
and worries, and even space and time, vanish like a dream, and are
replaced by the brightness of wisdom which enables him to understand the living meanings of important Ch'an idioms such as *host*
and *guest*, *substance* and *function*, *monkey mind* and *pure and clean
mind* etc. and to interpret correctly all Kung Ans, dialogues (Japanese, mondo) and Mahāyāna and Ch'an texts which are beyond the
reach of inexperienced beginners and outsiders.

As an illustration of this state of spiritual awakening, we present
the following English translation of a passage from a letter received
from a European Buddhist:

'. . . I then came to the passage of your translation which became
so important for me: "Q. How to escape from birth and death?
R. What is the use of escaping? Q. How to avoid them? R. That one
has neither birth nor death."[1] Suddenly this direct answer from
master Hui Ts'ang caused an indescribable commotion within me.
I felt as if a heavy cloak had suddenly dropped from my shoulders,
and found myself floating—I do not know where, in the void without any support. Moreover, I felt myself like a bright white light
similar to white snow without knowing whether it was within or
without, and all this enchantment of a crystalline white vibrated in

[1] Cf *Ch'an and Zen Teaching, First Series*, p. 137. Rider, London.

absolute silence, the sole sound of which was joy; this silent sound was only felt but could not be heard, because it was like the *silence of snow.* There were no eyes to see the light; it was rather that light which saw itself. In short, an intense visual feeling, the sound of which was absolute silence. I think I had an experience of the living formless light which is the root of all forms, although essentially free from them all.... I cannot say how long this wonderful experience lasted, perhaps a second, perhaps an hour, as I did not even care to look at the clock.... Then after this indescribable joy, there remained in my mind-heart only peace or rather serenity the sweetness and deepness of which were beyond all description, like the previous light; and while in this state, I again became conscious and looked in front of me. I remained so for a long while.... After that everything returned to normal, that is to its worldly condition.... I was then seized with a foolish desire to dance, jump and cry out, but overcame it not without difficulty. I then experienced a flash (vajra) of the same light (which was ultrarapid this second time) followed by the same profound and sweet serenity. However, this time I could observe its process which I now am able to reproduce at will, and this is most wonderful. Moreover I have gained the impression that it was the recreative condition of Death itself; so I no more fear death.... You are the second person on earth who knows of my experience which you have correctly predicted.... I abhor publicity and stupid congratulation....'

In another letter the same European friend wrote: 'Happy are those who will understand this marvellous passage of your translation.... I really needed it, and this time the gods have really guided your hand. Moreover, I was convinced long ago that if this famous "Transmission of the Lamp", the best document available in Asia, were translated, it would do an immense good.... Here, I say "yes" all your translations are perfectly clear and intelligible, taking into account that this comprehension can only belong to a person already familiarised with Buddhist terms in general. But today in the West there are such people to whom your work will prove very profitable —20 years earlier, no ...'

In his third letter he wrote: 'I trust you have received my previous

letter giving a rapid outline of my happy experience of which you
are one of the causes, the determinant one. Let me explain: nobody
is the cause of fire but if one rubs two pieces of wood one becomes
the determinant cause of the manifestation of fire. Or if you like I
was a heap of straw and you unintentionally approached with a
burning match and then puff . . . The straw caught fire because it
was dry and its dryness came from my studies and efforts—a preceding cause, like the fire latent in the two pieces of wood before they
are rubbed. The primal cause rests with the doctrine of the Buddha
who is the causeless cause. . . .'

Kung ans also consist of giving a shout, a loud roar of laughter or
a blow with a staff; of showing two hands wide open; of raising a
finger; of holding up a cake or a cup of tea; and of other gesticula-
tions, as presented in the second volume of our Ch'an and Zen
Teaching series (Rider, London), to teach the students to return the
mind's functionings to their source, that is the mind itself, in accord-
ance with the teaching on *Substance* (t'i) and *Function* (yung).[1]

Readers will find in Part III of this volume a translation of Master
Chi Ch'eng's *Ch'an Shout* which reveals the living meaning of this
kind of kung an.

(C) THE HUA T'OU TECHNIQUE AND THE FEELING OF DOUBT

When men were more attached to material things, people of high
spirituality became rare. The masters were then obliged to devise a
poison-against-poison method called Hua T'ou which consists of
giving rise to a feeling of doubt (i-ch'ing) about WHO the seeker of
Enlightenment is. Emphasis is on the word WHO which supports this
vital doubt which comes from the student's eagerness to know that
which practises the Dharma. He knows that his body and intellect
will cease to exist when he dies and are, therefore, transient and
cannot realise permanent reality. He is keen to know about the prime
mover of all his activities; hence his doubt which, growing larger
and larger, will submerge his body, mind and environment to form
a mass of fire which destroys all thoughts, feelings and passions like

[1] Cf *Ch'an and Zen Teaching, Second Series*, p. 64. Rider, London.

a red-hot stove which melts the snow that falls on it, as the masters put it. His monkey mind cannot stay in this scorching fire, and its death is automatically followed by the resurrection of his true mind which is pure and clean. This i-ch'ing should be maintained throughout the training until Bodhi is achieved.

After the student has wiped out all dualities in their coarse aspects, he will reach the state of bright stillness which still implies awareness of it, that is a duality of subjective ego and objective dhyāna in its subtlety. They are ego and Dharma in their finest aspects mentioned in the sūtras as the last hindrance on the holy path.

It is much easier to relinquish the subtle ego than the subtle Dharma which is wonderful and attractive, and can be easily mistaken for Nirvāṇa. Hence master Han Shan says: 'This is the most dangerous pass which I have myself experienced.'[1] If the student persists in holding on to this feeling of doubt, this subtle Dharma which is but an illusion will vanish, and thus released from the last hindrance, he will leap over both phenomenon and noumenon to reach that state of samādhi in which the i-ch'ing itself is sublimated and transformed into the Buddha's all-knowledge (sarvajña). This is the Tathāgata stage.

Therefore, the i-ch'ing or feeling of doubt plays the same role of chih and kuan simultaneously by stopping all rising thoughts and by staying alert so as not to slip into dullness and confusion for the purpose of looking into the mind which is no more stirred by sense data. It is an ingenious device which is most effective in Ch'an training.

This feeling of doubt, which the masters likened to an indestructible sword, cuts down all thoughts and mental states during the training. Hence Lin Chi says: 'If you meet a Buddha, cut him down; if you meet a Patriarch, cut him down; if you meet an arhat, cut him down; if you meet your parents, cut them down; and if you meet your relatives, cut them down. Only thus will you be liberated, and if you are not held by externals, you will be disengaged and comfortably independent.'[2] For all visions conceived by sense organs are

[1] Cf *The Secrets of Chinese Meditation*, p. 58. Rider, London.
[2] Cf *Ch'an and Zen Teaching, Second Series*, p. 125. Rider, London.

B

unreal and can never compare to the inconceivable and inexpressible Bhūtatathatā.

I give the following excerpt from a letter from an English Buddhist about the feeling of doubt:

'In view of a remark you make in the preface to *Chinese Meditation* about Westerners who have made some advances in dhyana practice, you might be interested to hear about the following experience which certainly changed my complete life. It will confirm, I believe, that when a living guru is not available sometimes a book can give the required help. Though in this case it was not actually one of your books for it took place some years ago before we had them. . . .

'From *Tibetan Yoga* I took as my guide the yoga of Mahāmudrā. For many, many hours I sat in meditation; at first with very little success for my legs were always stiff and ached and never for a moment would the thoughts that crowded my mind stop. But slowly over the weeks and then the months a change took place; though I was to go through a stage when I was so sick of the seeking. A great misery would cloud my mind and I thought I was going mad. I could not meditate; my arms and legs ached, my head was as if on fire, I could not eat or sleep, I felt my life was useless and that there was no way out; I came even to hate everything about the Dharma and the doubt in my mind was "what if the Dharma is all a lie?". All I could do was lie about in misery, lost to the beauty about me; then I would go down to the sea and swim far out telling myself I would end it all, I would just swim till I could swim no more and then sink. But then I would become afraid of death and turn and struggle back to land.

'There was one thought though that never came into my mind, and that was that I should leave and give the whole search up. So back in the end I would go to meditation; till in the end I found I wanted more and more to sit in meditation and had to make myself take exercises or rest. During this period I was sitting one night in meditation on the rock like a seat that was near my tent, when I felt that the whole rock with me on it rose into the air; suddenly there was nothing but space all round me, for looking down I could not see the earth below. We were out in space with only the stars about us, the rock and I. It gave me a great fright but I clung to the thought that it was an illusion; just as when lights had danced before my eyes or shapes had formed. But this time the illusion was more vivid than any that had gone before. I then thought that perhaps I was mad for I could no longer be sure what was in my mind and what was not; but all the time I kept my mind on the question "who" sees things, "who" is it sitting here, "who" is it that is conscious? I knew this was a stage I must pass.

'Then one night when there was a lovely full moon, in my second year on the cliffs, I felt I could not sleep. For days I had been in one of my periods of doubt and misery: I really was in need of some one I could discuss this thing with, but of course there was no one. In this state of mind I started to walk along the coast by a path I had never been on before. For hours I walked not knowing or caring where I went, often stumbling where shadow hid the moonlight on the path. My head was throbbing with the one question, "who am I . . . who is this moving . . . who . . . who?". Except for this one question it seemed that my mind was a frozen block of doubt and misery and question, it seemed to weigh down, to press my whole body down so that I stumbled under the weight and my feet felt like lead, as if in a dream. How long I walked or how far I have no idea, but gradually I became aware that the landscape had changed. I was no longer walking on cliffs or moors above the sea; now trees and bamboos were spreading overhead and strange plants were growing beside the path, and the path itself had changed. Instead of the rough track it had become flagged with large round slabs of stone.

'Rounding a bend in this strange pathway I saw before me a small lake with bamboos hanging over the water . . . a few steps and I came to an arched wooden bridge and I suddenly knew I was in a Japanese garden. But here in England . . . it must be another hallucination or I am really in a dream. As if dazed, not sure of anything, I stand and stare; the moonlight was reflected on the water and I watched the silver disks move among large water plants; there was the scent of strange flowers on the air and I could hear the distant tinkle of a bell. The bridge I saw crossed over to a small island in the middle of the lake, and feeling as if all self-will had been drained from my body, I felt myself moving over the bridge.

'I crossed to the island and saw what had before been hidden by the thick bamboos . . . there on a rock sat the Enlightened One, the Buddha, silvery white in the moonlight. At that moment it was as if where a moment before there was something with a shell of misery and doubt about it was suddenly no more. It was gone and there was only a radiance of bliss and peace and vast space. . . . When self-consciousness returned I became aware first that a pale golden light was spreading through the trees overhead, while under me I could feel the cold hardness of stone on which I lay; I did not know where I was or who I was and it did not seem to be important. I just sat there looking at a world that had that moment been born. The Buddha rupa, carved in stone, sat in meditation, turning golden in the early morning sunlight that came through the bamboos; it was at the base of the Buddha rupa that I sat, on a flat stone. But of much greater interest was the life about me; flowers alive with light, each leaf burning with life, the sunlight on the water a brilliance seen for the first time, the feeling of the stone and moss seemed to fill the whole field of consciousness. It was as if consciousness that perceived all these was located, not in this body, but saw from a point that was the middle; it saw but also felt itself the leaf, the flower, the water, the rock, and also at this moment it felt everything was being created, everything was in the state of "is". But of any sense of an "I" that saw all this there was none.

'In that state I found my body lightly walking on, as if hardly touching the ground, and later that morning I was back at my tent. This new way of seeing everything lasted like this for some days; also the strange feeling of lightness as if my body was without weight. I had no wish to speak to any one; in fact I kept out of the way so that I did not have to meet any one. And time seemed to stand still. So much wonder to be gazed at.

'From that memorable night I knew that the way is always here and now; the great problem was not so great after all. It is this mind that makes a shell of thoughts to encase something that is nothing that is called "self". Then this self makes a hell of this earth. So why go off to Ceylon; here and now is enough for the great purpose. For after all the problem always goes with the going; stay here and drop it. I don't think there is much more that can be said at this stage, but there is a great deal more to be done. . . .

'Forgive this long letter and once again let me thank you for the great deal of valuable help your books have been; my guru between hard covers.'

Readers will find in the above passage that the English Buddhist succeeded in giving rise to a great doubt that caused his spiritual awakening (wu in Chinese and satori in Japanese) although he was completely unaware of it when he felt his mind was a 'frozen block of misery and doubt and question'. Is it not a case of ch'an training in his previous life which he now resumed in a country where conditions are favourable for his great leap after a disastrous war? Had someone told him beforehand about these feelings he would have clung to form and name and would have failed. This is why the ancient masters did not disclose the profound meanings of their sayings to prevent their disciples from thinking and discriminating.

The Stages of Realisation
According to the Teaching School, a devotee should pass through three asankhyeyas or innumerable kalpas (aeons) before achieving bodhi: the first to hear about the Dharma, the second to practise it and the third to realise it. The sūtras mention fifty-six stages of Bodhisattva development into Buddhahood, but the Ch'an sect, which is a shortcut to Enlightenment, wipes out the time element thereby ensuring instantaneous illumination. Hence master Kao Feng says: 'When a student looks into a hua t'ou with the same steadiness with which a broken tile, when thrown into a deep pond, plunges straight down to the bottom, if he fails to become awakened in seven days, any one can chop off my head and take it away.'[1]

For Ch'an formulates only correct interpretation of subject and object, substance and function and host and guest with their integra-

[1] Cf *Ch'an and Zen Teaching, First Series*, p. 24. Rider, London.

tion into the undivided whole or the absolute from which both the
real and the unreal arise. This consists of wiping out first the coarse
objective sense data and then the coarse subjective sense organs by
means of the agony of doubt, a sharp weapon that cuts down both
and exposes their voidness or unreality. After that, the subjective
awareness of the void should be disengaged from its object with the
same technique. When the void ceases to exist, the subjective ego is
replaced by a subtle awareness of the all-embracing state of voidness which can be easily mistaken for Nirvāṇa. Thus the devotee
returns to the primordial state of the mind when it was stirred by the
first thought since time without beginning, and is likened to a man
who sits on the top of a hundred-foot pole from which he should
make a step forward to achieve bodhi, or to a man who carries on
his head a board which he should throw away in order not to be
hindered by it. But if this is mistaken for Nirvāṇa, it implies the
subtle subjective ego and its objective realisation or Dharma, which
are the two last hindrances which should be overcome with the
same i-ch'ing technique. At this stage it is easier to wipe out the
subtle ego than the subtle Dharma for the latter is so wonderful and
so attractive that it cannot be easily relinquished. This is precisely
ālaya which eminent Taoists in China regarded as the ultimate for
they failed to transmute it into the Great Mirror Wisdom as they
had not had the good fortune to meet the Buddha.

This is why Lin Chi says: 'Followers of the Tao, it is most important for you to seek the correct interpretation, and then you can
walk freely in every direction all over the world; your bodies and
minds will be no more disturbed by fox sprites who give wrong
hints and talk nonsense. You should refrain from creating anything
and be just ordinary for as soon as you stir your minds for something else you are already wrong. Moreover, do not seek Buddha
for Buddha is only a name and a term, but do you know who this
seeker of Buddha is?'[1]

Correct interpretation involves the devotee's line of conduct,
that is his deed, word and thought which should accord with the
Host; it is vital in ch'an practice, especially in this Dharma ending

[1] Cf *Ch'an and Zen Teaching, Second Series,* p. 115. Rider, London.

age when the teaching is so distorted that he can be easily deceived by the unauthentic versions and misleading commentaries which are found everywhere. Hence Lin Chi says: 'Nowadays, students of Ch'an do not know the Dharma; they are like a goat nosing any-thing which it immediately takes in its mouth. They do not distin-guish a servant from a master and a guest from a host. These people who enter the Tao with perverted minds cannot be called true leavers of home; they are really householders (i.e. worldlings). True leavers of home should know what is the ordinary and correct interpretation; should distinguish Buddha from demon, the real from the unreal and the worldly from the saintly. If they can make these distinctions, they are called true leavers of home. If they can-not distinguish demon from Buddha, they are like a man who leaves one home to enter another; they are called karma-producing living beings. . . . Now if there be a Buddha and a demon appearing in one body, a follower of the Tao who has a deep insight will cut down both Buddha and demon. If you like the saintly and dislike the worldly, you will float and sink in the sea of birth and death with no end in sight.'[1]

The great masters were reluctant to use words and terms found in the sūtras when giving instruction to their disciples lest the latter might cling to them and so neglect the real aim of the Mind Transmission. They used words and terms of the vocabulary of the Uncreate such as: it, this one, that one, host and guest, subject and object, prince and minister, substance and function, the moon and the cold pool, the first, second and third rate meanings, the master's last word, etc. to cut off the pupils' discrimination and block every exit so that their monkey minds could not wander outside and could be brought under control.

The master's duty is to discover his student's weak points and to guide and adjust his potentiality so that it can absorb and unite with the Tao. Hence Lin Chi says: 'Sometimes the subject is snatched away but the object is not; sometimes the object is snatched away but the subject is not; sometimes both subject and object are snatched away; and sometimes neither subject nor object is

[1] Cf Ch'an and Zen Teaching, Second Series, pp. 116-17. Rider, London.

snatched away.'[1] However, in the absence of competent masters in
this Dharma ending age, the student can adjust the various stages of
his meditation with the instructions given by the seven founders of
the Five Ch'an sects which we have presented in the second volume
of our *Ch'an and Zen Teaching* series (Rider, London). He will find
that his progress goes deeper and deeper in each more advanced
stage, and will gain newer and newer experience when passing
from the coarsest to the finest illusions of ego and dharma.

The Heart of Stone

The devotee can make correct interpretation only if he relinquishes
all worldly attachments. If he is firmly determined to get out of the
realm of illusion and suffering, he should give up the three main
passions: carnality, killing and stealing, which are considered by all
worldlings as most important in life and which are the chief causes
of birth and death according to *The Śūraṅgama Sūtra*. For carnality
is the *raison d'être* of existence in saṁsāra; killing is to provide food to
preserve this existence; and stealing is to rob the flesh of other living
beings to obtain that food. After he has succeeded in refraining from
these three evils, he will be able to develop a *Heart of Stone* which no
water of love can soak and no fire of passion to kill and steal can
scorch. He will be indifferent to sense data and will be immune
from contamination by them. He will see clearly, will be able to
distinguish between the real and the unreal, and will encounter no
serious hindrance in his practice.

The Spiritual Master (Guru)

Lin Chi says: 'In your red heart there is a true man of no fixed
position who comes in and out through your forehead; I urge those
who have not experienced this to try to see it.'[2] This *true man* is the
spiritual master or guru inherent in man's heart or mind but
screened by ignorance. If the student succeeds in stopping the flow
of thoughts to still his mind and at the same time refrains from the
above-mentioned three passions, the good roots or excellent

[1] Cf *Ch'an and Zen Teaching, Second Series,* pp. 92–3. Rider, London.
[2] Cf *Ch'an and Zen Teaching, Second Series,* p. 110. Rider, London.

qualities of his inner guru will manifest as described by master Chih I, the Fourth Patriarch of the T'ien T'ai School.[1] But the ego which the student treasured before is still very strong, being sustained by the force of habits contracted since time without beginning; it will refuse to concede defeat to his inner guru who barely appears and is still very weak.

The battle between ego and guru may be long or short. If the student is not spiritually strong enough or is of wavering faith, his ego will certainly defeat his inner guru who still has no strength to assert himself. The student will give up his practice and return to the worldly way of life. Hence we have seen people who were very enthusiastic about the Dharma at the beginning but who gradually became lukewarm and finally dropped its practice.

It is most important that the student should never allow desire, anger and stupidity to slip into the field of meditation. Any one of them will grow out of all proportion when inadvertently concentrated upon and will be very difficult to root out. For instance, a meditator may become unreasonably irate if he allows himself to be displeased with some unimportant matter during his meditation, and his least thought of desire or love may become so exaggerated and so uncontrollable that it may cause him to commit evil acts he never dreamt of before. Hence the Chinese saying: 'When the Tao grows a foot, the demon is already ten feet high.' This is why the masters always urge their disciples to hold on to the feeling of doubt to prevent evil thoughts from slipping into the field of meditation.

If the student is firm in his faith, is determined to get out of saṁsāra and is strongly supported by his great vow to deliver others, that is if he is well sustained by his Bodhisattva compassion for all living beings, he will make rapid progress, and his inner guru will grow stronger and will defeat his ego which will vanish like a dream. Henceforth his spiritual master will watch, criticise, scold and correct him when he inadvertently strays from the holy Path. But the inner guru just out of the veil of ignorance is still inexperienced and is not mature enough when confronting wondrous states which usually precede illumination. In other words, fine traces of

[1] Cf *The Secrets of Chinese Meditation*, p. 139. Rider, London.

ignorance still exist. It is here that the student should guard against the fifty mental states which we have mentioned earlier. If he is firmly determined to fulfil his Bodhisattva vow, it will merge into the strong vows of past Buddhas and Bodhisattvas, and will become invincible, and thereby remove all remaining obstructions to the full manifestation of his spiritual master who will force him to come out into the open to enlighten and deliver all living beings.

The spiritual master is but the student's inherent Buddha-nature which is no more screened by ignorance, and whose two characteristics, Samādhi (imperturbability) and Prajñā (wisdom), are now in perfect working condition, Samādhi being its substance and Prajñā its function.

PART II

The Story of the Third Ch'an Patriarch of China and his gāthā 'Have Faith In Your Mind' (Hsin Hsin Ming)

From 'The Transmission of the Lamp'
Translated by Upāsaka Lu K'uan Yü (Charles Luk)

AFTER Hui K'o had succeeded Bodhidharma as the Second Patriarch of China, he continued to spread the doctrine of the Mind, looking at the same time for a successor to his Dharma and robe.

One day a upāsaka who was over forty years of age came to pay reverence to Hui K'o; without disclosing his name, he said: 'I suffer from bad rheumatism and beg the Venerable Sir to teach me how to repent my sins.' Hui K'o said: 'Show me your sins and I shall teach you.' After a long pause, the visitor declared: 'I cannot find my sins.' Hui K'o said: 'Then I have taught you how to repent them. You should take refuge in the Buddha, the Dharma and the Saṅgha.' The visitor asked: 'As I now see, you are the Saṅgha, but what are Buddha and Dharma?' Hui K'o replied: 'Mind is Buddha and Mind is Dharma. Buddha and Dharma are not a duality; nor is Saṅgha (in relation to either of them).' The visitor said: 'Today for the first time I know that sins are neither within nor without nor in between, and that Buddha and Dharma are not a duality but just (the non-dual) mind.'

Hui K'o held the visitor in high esteem and then shaved his head, saying: 'You are my jewel and should be called Seng Ts'an (i.e. The Lustre of Saṅgha).' That year on the eighteenth of the third month, Seng Ts'an received full ordination at Kuang Fu temple. He recovered gradually from his illness and stayed with Hui K'o as his attendant for two years. One day his master said: 'I inherited the right Dharma Eye from Bodhidharma who came from distant India, and now transmit it to you, together with his robe as a token of faith. You should guard them carefully without allowing the Teaching to be discontinued. Now listen to my gāthā:

> From the seed-bed (of your mind)
> (The Dharma) raises flowers.
> Yet there is no seed
> Nor are there flowers.'

After the transmission of the Dharma and robe, Hui K'o said: 'You have now inherited my Dharma. Go and live deep in the mountains, this is not the time to spread the Dharma because there will soon be a national disaster.'

Seng Ts'an then went to stay on Huan Kung Shan Mountain at Shu Chou (in Anhwei Province). When emperor Wu Ti of the Pei Chou dynasty (557–9) ordered the destruction of Buddhism, nobody knew of Seng Ts'an's whereabouts as he wandered from place to place between T'ai Hu Hsien district and Szu K'ung Shan Mountain. In the twelfth year (592–3) of the emperor K'ai Huang of the Sui dynasty, a fourteen-year-old monk named Tao Hsin called on him and later succeeded him as the Fourth Patriarch of China.

After the transmission of the Dharma and robe to Tao Hsin, Seng Ts'an went to Lo Fu mountain where he stayed for two years, after which he returned to his former place. A month later the literati and people came and made offerings to him. He taught them the Mind Dharma, and on the fifteenth of the tenth month of the second year (606) of Ta Yeh, after he had expounded the Dharma under a large tree, he brought his palms together and passed away while standing.

Seng Ts'an wrote the following gāthā:

Have Faith in Your Mind
(Hsin Hsin Ming)

It is not hard to realise your Mind
Which should not be an object of your choice.
Throw like and dislike away
And you'll be clear about it.
The slightest deviation from it means
A gulf as deep as that 'twixt heaven and earth.

If you want it to manifest
Be not for or against a thing,
For that is contentious,
A disease of the mind.
If its profoundness you ignore
You can never practise stillness.
Perfect like the great void it lacks
Nothing and has naught in excess.
If you discriminate
You will miss its suchness.
To external causes cling not, stay
Not in the void (that is relative).
If you can be impartial
Differentiation ceases.
To stop disturbance leads to stillness
Which, if clung to, stirs the mind. But if
To opposites you cling
How can you know the One?
If you do not recognise One Mind
Two opposites will lead you nowhere.
To avoid what *is* means to cling to what *is not*,
To cling to what *is not* means to revive what *is*.
The more you talk and think,
The further are you from it.
If you can halt all speech and thought
You will find it everywhere.
If you think success means to return all things to their source,
You will differ (from our Sect) by clinging to its function.[1]
The moment that you look within
You surpass your contemplation
Of the void which is always changing
Due to your discriminating views.

[1] If you think that your goal can be reached by returning all things to the root, i.e. the mind, you will cling to its function and will err from our Ch'an sect which is beyond the notion of functioning. Cf *Ch'an and Zen Teaching, Third Series*, p. 70, line 22. Rider, London.

Do not seek the real
But your false views lay down.
Avoid the real and the false
And never search for either.
Once you start to choose between what's right and wrong,
You will become confused and will lose your Mind.
All pairs from the One Mind spring
Which never should be clung to.
If the One Mind does not stir
Then all things will be harmless.
Things that are harmless cease to be,
Mind that stirs not does not exist.
Subjects disengaged from objects vanish,
Objects like their creator disappear.
Objects are caused by subjects
On whose existence they depend.
If you would understand dualities
Know that they spring from Voidness absolute.
The absolute and all dualities
Are one, from it all things originate.
When you cease choosing between the coarse
And fine all prejudices die.
Since the Great Mind embraces all,
To realise it is not difficult
Or easy. In their distrust the ignorant
Waver between eagerness and hesitation.
If you grasp at it, you will be in the wrong
Falling into the way of heretics.
If you lay it down
It stays not nor goes.
With the Tao unite your nature
And you will be free from troubles.
Clinging from the real strays
And to confusion leads.
Discrimination's useless
So weary not your mind.

If you want to know the One
Reject not six sense data.
If they're not rejected
They are one with Bodhi.
The wise man is non-active,
The ignorant bind themselves.
All things are the same at heart
But clinging's from delusion.
If mind is used to seek itself,
Is this not a grave mistake?
Delusion brings stillness and disturbance;
Bodhi is far beyond all good and evil.
All the pairs of opposites
From discrimination come.
Dreams, illusions and flowers in
The sky are not worth attachment.
Gain and loss, and right and wrong
Should be laid down now at once.
If your eyes close not in sleep
All your dreams will disappear.
If you do not discriminate,
Then all things will be as they are.
Profound is this state of suchness,
Lofty and beyond illusions.
If things are not thought different,
To their nature they will return.
When they disappear,
Mind's without compare.
When it stops moving disturbance is no more;
When all motion ceases, stillness also stops.
When opposites disappear,
Where then can the One Mind be?
When for the Ultimate you search,
You find it has no pattern.
In this impartial mind
Duality has vanished.

When distrust ceases,
Your faith will be true.
When all is thrown away
There's nothing to remember.
The Mind that now is pure
Radiates and is not tired.
Since it is beyond discriminative thinking
It cannot be fathomed by that which knows and feels.
Such is the state absolute
Free from the self and others.
If you would be one with it
All duality avoid.
In all places the non-dual is
The same and there is naught outside it.
Sages everywhere
To this sect belong,
Which is beyond time, long or short,
For a thought lasts ten thousand years.
It neither *is* nor *is not*
For everywhere is here.
The smallest equals the largest
For it is not confined by space.
The largest equals the smallest
For it is not within, without.
Is and *is not* are the same,
For what *is not* equals *is*.
If you cannot so awaken
Then you should change your ways.
Now One is All
And All is One.
If you can so awaken,
Why worry if you do not win it?
Just believe that your Mind is non-dual
For your Faith in it is not divided.
In it there's no room for word and speech;
It has no present, past or future.

PART III

The Ch'an Shout

By CH'AN MASTER CHI CH'ENG

From The Imperial Selection of Ch'an Sayings
Translated by Upāsaka Lu K'uan Yü (Charles Luk)

CH'AN master Chi Ch'eng and three eminent Ch'an masters, Yuan Wu, Fa Chen and Tz'u Shou, were invited to a vegetarian dinner at governor Ch'en Liang P'i's residence where ten learned Dharma-masters and a thousand monks of the Ch'an Sect and of other schools were also present. Emperor Huei Tsung of the Sung dynasty (1101–26) availed himself of the occasion to come incognito to listen to their discussions.

There was among the guests a Dharma-master who was well versed in the Hua Yen (Avataṁsaka) teaching and was regarded as a skilful interpreter of (Patriarch) Hsien Shou's doctrine. Said he to the guests: 'The Buddha set up a Dharma which consists in wiping out gradually, from the stage of Hīnayāna to that of Perfect Teaching, all concepts of *is* and *is not* to realise permanence for the achievement of myriads of sublime virtues and the final attainment of Buddhahood. I have heard that a mere Ch'an shout can turn worldlings into saints; this seems to contradict the sūtras and treatises. If a shout can pass through all the five stages of our Hua Yen School, I shall concede that it is right, otherwise it is just heresy.'

All the Ch'an monks looked at Chi Ch'eng who said: 'The Venerable Dharma-master's query does not require an answer from the three great Ch'an masters, and though I am the youngest among them, I shall be able to clear away his delusion.' He then called the Dharma-master who answered: 'Yes.' Chi Ch'eng said: 'According to the Venerable Sir's interpretation of the Hua Yen Teaching,

Hīnayāna deals with existence; Mahāyāna in its primary stage, with non-existence; Mahāyāna in its final stage, with the doctrine of neither existence nor non-existence; the Sudden School, with the identity of existence and non-existence; and the Perfect Teaching, with reality without existence yet existing and without non-existence yet non-existent. As to our sect's One Shout, it can pass through not only these five Hua Yen stages, but also all kinds of arts, crafts and philosophies.'

He then gave a thundering shout and asked the Dharma-master: 'Did you hear?' The Dharma-master replied: 'Yes.' Chi Ch'eng said: 'As you heard it, it stands for *is* and passes through the Hīnayāna teaching.'

A little later, he said: 'Do you hear?' The Dharma-master replied: 'I do not.' Chi Ch'eng said: 'If you do not hear, it stands for *is not* and passes through the Mahāyāna's primary stage.'

He then looked at the Dharma-master and said: 'At first, when I gave a shout, you said you heard it, and as my voice has vanished, you now say you do not hear it. When you say that it *is not* heard now, it really *was* heard before and when you said that it *was* heard before, it *is not* now. So that which neither *is* nor *is not* passes through the Mahāyāna's final stage.

'When I first gave a shout, its existence was not really existence for it is its (present) non-existence that reveals its (previous) existence. As I do not give a shout now, its non-existence is not really non-existence for it was its (previous) existence that revealed its (present) non-existence. This is identity of *is* and *is not* and passes through the Sudden School.

'You should know that that shout of mine is (now) not used as a shout[1] and is beyond both *is* and *is not*. It is above all feeling and explanation. When you speak of *is*, it does not set up a particle of dust and when you speak of *is not*, it embraces boundless space. It intermingles with hundreds, thousands, tens of thousands and hundreds of thousands of shouts; hence its ability to pass through the Perfect Teaching.'

[1] Cf *Ch'an and Zen Teaching, Second Series*, pp. 96–7 for detailed explanation of Lin Chi's four kinds of Shouts.

Thereupon the Dharma-master rose from his seat to bow his thanks. Chi Ch'eng continued: 'Not only can this shout pass through the five Hua Yen stages, but even speech, silence, motion and stillness, all time from the past to the present, boundless space in the ten directions, the vast variety of phenomena, the six realms of existence and four forms of birth, all Buddhas of the three times, and Saints and Sages, the 84,000 Dharma-doors to Enlightenment, hundreds and thousands of states of Samādhi, and countless profound meanings, all of which accord with the noumenon and fundamental quality, and are of the same substance as all phenomena in the universe; this is the Dharmakāya. As the three realms of existence come from the Mind and all things are created by Consciousness, the uniformity of the four seasons and of the eight annual divisions[1] and the sameness of the positive and negative principles are called the nature of Dharma (Dharmatā). Hence the Avataṁsaka Sūtra says: "The nature of Dharma is omnipresent; the material and the immaterial as well as sound and form are contained in a particle of dust which comprises the four profound meanings."[2] The unimpeded interaction of noumenon and phenomenon obtains everywhere for they enter each other without differentiation, and mix with each other without unity; all this is covered by this One Shout. But this is still an expedient set up to convert people and serves as a temporary rest, for they have not yet arrived at the Treasure House. For you are not clear about our Patriarch's sect which aims at Transmission from Mind to Mind, and Sealing of Dharma by Dharma, without setting up Scriptures, for the perception of self-nature and attainment of Buddhahood. There still is the Upward Path[3] which no Saints will transmit to you.'

The Dharma-master asked: 'What is the Upward Path?' Chi Ch'eng replied: 'Look down to awaken to it.' The Dharma-master

[1] The four seasons, two equinoxes and two solstices.

[2] According to the Hua Yen Teaching, the realm of Dharma (Dharmadhātu) comprises: (a) the phenomenal realm, with differentiation; (b) the noumenal realm, with unity; (c) the realm of both the noumenal and phenomenal which are interdependent; and (d) the realm of phenomena which are also interdependent.

[3] The Upward Path is the Transcendental Path. To look up and down is a

asked: 'What is the Treasure House?' Chi Ch'eng replied: 'This state is beyond your reach.' The Dharma-master said: 'May the Venerable Ch'an Master be compassionate enough to reveal it to me.' Chi Ch'eng replied:

'Even the ocean may undergo a change
But I shall never disclose it to you.'

The Dharma-master was speechless and then left. The emperor was greatly pleased with Chi Ch'eng's erudition which was admired by all those present.

Ch'an idiom. To look down is to look into externals which spring from the mind and trace them back to their source for realisation of self-mind and perception of self-nature. To look up is to look into the Absolute which is inexpressible and beyond the comprehension of worldlings. It is, therefore, futile to teach the Absolute which is indescribable and can be realised only by personal experience; hence Chi Ch'eng says: 'No Saints will transmit it to you' and 'I shall never disclose it to you'.

PART IV

Master Han Shan's Experiment with the Mind

BEFORE dealing with master Han Shan's experiment with Ch'an meditation, we should know that the Mind should be the point of departure in our spiritual training for the purpose of getting out of the realm of illusion and suffering. For the mind creates all things, is conditioned by our way of thinking and can cause our incarnation in either heaven, earth, hell and other worlds of existence. The capacity of the mind can be reduced to that of a particle of dust or expanded to fill the immensity of boundless space. The mind of a pickpocket does not go beyond the size of his victim's purse; that of the cinema goer does not exceed the screen on which the pictures are projected; that of a hunter is reduced to the form of the bird he aims at; that of a murderer is confined to the body of his victim; that of a greedy person is restricted to the sum of money he covets; and that of a gambler is limited to the roulette wheel in a casino. The mind of a lover is conditioned by his sweetheart's features, and the French novelist Gustave Flaubert ably described Dr. Bovary's universe which did not go beyond the corners of the skirt of his unfaithful wife.

In his practice of meditation, the moment a devotee ceases thinking his mind is free from all bondage; the moment he stops discriminating and discerning, it is free from all dualities, relativities and contraries, does not abide anywhere, and grows larger and larger until it becomes all-embracing like boundless space. If he also cultivates uncaused compassion for all living beings, its functioning will be impartial, beneficial and far-reaching. Since his mind is boundless, it is everywhere and perceives everything; hence the Buddha's omnipresence and omniscience.

The Reading of the Autobiography of master Han Shan is most rewarding for all serious students of the Buddha-Dharma, especially for keen followers of the Transmission of Mind. The master was of exceptionally high spirituality and was fortunate to have a virtuous mother who, in spite of his father's opposition, did all she could to satisfy his early wish to join the Saṅgha.

Even at the tender age of seven, he was already keen to enquire about the question of birth and death when his uncle died and when the latter's son was born. As to his education, his mother was very strict and did her best to cut off his worldly feeling and affection so that he could later observe the rules of discipline.

The master's good karma also helped him to hear about the teaching of Avalokiteśvara Bodhisattva who was well known all over the country for his boundless compassion. At the age of ten, his chat with his mother showed his contempt for worldly heights and his keenness to leave home in his quest of the Truth. A happy incident brought him face to face with a few journeying monks who came to his house begging for food. At twelve, at his own request, he was sent to Pao En monastery where he had the first chance to meet its old abbot Hsi Lin who, during his lifetime, never discontinued his study and recitation of *The Diamond Sūtra*. He also met the eminent master Yun Ku who urged him to give up all worldly pursuits so as to devote all his time to Ch'an practice for realising the mind. As instructed by Yun Ku, he read *The Sayings of Chung Feng* (1263–1323) which prompted him to join the Order.

HIS FIRST PRACTICE OF PURE LAND MEDITATION

At nineteen, he did not know the Ch'an method of practice and concentrated his mind on repeating Amitābha's name. His pointed concentration soon resulted in his visions of the Three Holy Ones of the Western Paradise. Most beginners would be satisfied with the result, and would vow to be reborn in Amitābha's Pure Land so as to receive further instruction from that Buddha and his two attendant Bodhisattvas for advanced training. But Han Shan realised that these visions still involved the duality of subject and object, and being an ambitious young man, he called on eminent masters for instruction on Ch'an meditation, a shortcut to Enlightenment.

When he listened to master Wu Chi's lectures on Ch'ing Liang's commentary on *The Avataṁsaka Sūtra* which formulates the four dharma-realms: the phenomenal, with differentiation; the noumenal, with unity; both noumenal and phenomenal being interdependent; and all phenomena also being interdependent, he immediately awakened to the profound meaning of the unobstructed inter-permeating and inter-merging of all things. He had a vision of Ch'ing Liang (now called the Five-Peaked) Mountain and vowed to visit the holy place where Ch'ing Liang, the Fourth Patriarch of the Avataṁsaka School had stayed in the T'ang dynasty.

HIS TURNING TO CH'AN MEDITATION

In his twentieth year, he was taught the Kung An: 'Who is repeating the Buddha's name?' and succeeded in realising singleness of thought which caused him to be unmindful of the assembly's presence and other daily activities for three consecutive months. After this long meditation, he succeeded in preserving this state of unmindfulness, and went out without noticing a single person in the crowded market-place, which showed his right concentration, a prerequisite to Ch'an training.

In his twenty-first year, that is a year after the death of the old abbot Hsi Lin, his monastery was destroyed by fire. He vowed to rebuild it; he then went north to practise the Dharma first waiting for the opportune time to raise funds for the purpose. At Tien Chih monastery where he listened to Wu Chi's lectures on *The Lotus Sūtra*, he met Miao Feng, a monk whose duty was to clean the latrines of the monastery and who later realised Enlightenment. He proposed that Miao Feng be his companion on his long journey but the latter did not like being disturbed and departed secretly.

At twenty-six, with a bowl, he went north, and when he arrived at Peking the following year, he met Miao Feng, and also called on master Hsiao Yen who asked him: 'Do you remember the road that led you here?' Han Shan's answer, 'Once trodden it vanished', showed that he had awakened to the Buddha's saying, 'One should develop a mind that does not abide anywhere', and won the old master's approval. This was his awakening to the illusion of space.

HIS FIRST EXPERIENCE OF THE STATE OF DHYĀNA

In his twenty-eighth year, he arrived at the Five Peak Mountain where he saw a mountain of strange beauty called Han Shan or The Silly Mountain; he took his second name after it; hence he was known as master Han Shan. However, he could not bear the bitter cold there and went first to Peking and then to P'an Shan Mountain on the top of which he found a hermit in a cave who refused to speak to him. Han Shan stayed in the cave, and one night went out for a walk. Suddenly his forehead burst with a noise like thunder; his body, mind and environment vanished in a flash. This state of still voidness lasted for about half an hour and gradually everything returned to normal. His body and mind became weightless and he experienced an indescribable bliss. When he related his experience to the hermit, the latter warned him against clinging to this manifestation of the aggregate of form which could hinder his quest of the Absolute.

Han Shan then left the cave and returned to Peking where, with Miao Feng, he again went to the Five Peak Mountain. Half-way to it, they met prefect Ch'en and decided to reprint *The Chao Lun*, a treatise by Séng Chao, an enlightened disciple of Kumārajīva. He was not clear about Seng Chao's teaching on the immutability of all phenomena, and as he now reread the text at the age of twenty-nine, he suddenly awakened to it, and exclaimed: 'Now I can believe that fundamentally all things neither come nor go.' He got off the meditation bed, prostrated himself before the Buddha shrine and did not have the perception of anything in motion. He went to the stone steps outside and stood there; suddenly the wind blew through the trees in the courtyard, and the air was filled with flying leaves which, however, looked motionless. He then went to the yard at the back to urinate, and the urine seemed not to be running. He said: 'This is why the river pours but does not flow.' Thereafter, all his doubts about birth and death vanished. This is also what the Sixth Patriarch meant when he said to two monks at Fa Hsin monastery at Canton: 'Neither the wind nor the banner moves; the minds of the Venerable Sirs really move.'[1]

He also met master Fa Kuang who said: 'Your practice should go beyond mind, intellect and consciousness; and your study should be above both the saintly and the worldly.' Fa Kuang also urged him to catch a living dragon (i.e. living Zen) instead of a dead snake (i.e. mouth Zen). In other words, he should take up the *host* position instead of the *guest* stand.

In his thirtieth year, he reached the Five Peak Mountain where he stayed at the Dragon Gate of the North Peak; the scenery resembled identically the vision he had had when he was nineteen after listening to Wu Chi's talk on *The Avataṁsaka Sūtra*. In his auto-biography he wrote: 'My body and mind were taken by surprise as if I were entering the Paradise of Bliss.' Miao Feng then left so that the master could practise Ch'an meditation alone.

HIS MAJOR AWAKENING (JAPANESE, SATORI)

By pointed concentration of mind, Han Shan achieved singleness of thought, but when a roaring gale blew or when the thaw set in causing torrents of water to roll down the mountains like thunder, he could not still his mind. Remembering Avalokiteśvara Bodhi-sattva's method of perfection which consisted in turning back the ears' function of hearing, he practised it and soon found that the noise was audible when thoughts stirred his mind and was in-audible when they ceased. One day he suddenly felt as if his body had vanished and heard the noise no more. From then on he succeeded in disengaging his faculty of hearing from all sounds and noises. Another day while standing he realised the state of Samādhi;

[1] Cf *Ch'an and Zen Teaching, Third Series*, p. 28. Rider, London.

his body and mind disappeared and were replaced by a great brightness, spheric and full, clear and still, like a huge round mirror containing all the mountains, rivers and great earth. Thereafter he
noticed a still serenity inside and outside his body and met no more
hindrance from sounds and forms. His rice cooker was covered with
a thick layer of dust and, being alone, he did not know how long he
had been in the state of Samādhi.

After his major awakening, as there were no enlightened masters
to confirm and testify to it, he opened *The Śūraṅgama Sūtra* to verify
his experience. As he had not listened previously to lectures on this
sūtra, he did not know its profound meaning. Now by using his
wisdom which had just manifested, he took eight full months to
obtain a complete understanding of the Buddha's teaching in it
without having a single doubt left. This sūtra is a most profound one
and even in China very few Buddhist monks and devotees understand it. Our English translation of it (published by Rider, London)
is based on master Han Shan's explanation and commentary.

HIS BODHISATTVA-WORK, CHAN ILLNESS
AND SECOND MAJOR AWAKENING

The master began his Bodhisattva-work of salvation immediately
after his first great awakening. Abbot Ta Fang of T'a Yuan temple
who had made arrangements for Han Shan's meditation on the
Five Peak Mountain was the victim of a false accusation, was found
guilty and sentenced to leave the Order and to return to lay life.
Han Shan called on the prefect and obtained Ta Fang's release. The
prefect retained the master at the prefecture and asked him to write
poems for the viceroy. When he found he could not refuse his host's
request, he opened a book of poetry to stimulate his thinking which
had come to a stop as a result of his meditation. With the thinking
process in action, words and sentences came to him so rapidly that
they could not be stopped. Remembering what Fa Kuang had told
him previously about his own Ch'an illness, he tried hard to sleep
but instead he entered the state of Samādhi which, after lasting five
successive days and nights, was interrupted by his host who woke

him up. He wrote in his autobiography: 'I sat silently and reflected carefully, but I failed to realise where I was and from whence I came. I looked back to my stay on the mountain and my past journeys, and all of those events were like things seen in a dream; after searching, nothing could be found in my mind. All that previously had been in tumult in the great void was now as still as when the rains had passed and all the clouds dispersed. The air seemed thoroughly cleansed and everything was perfectly tranquil without a single appearance of shadows or images. The mind was empty and the surrounding objects were still; the resultant bliss was without compare.' He repeated the following lines of Mañjuśrī's gāthā in *The Śūraṅgama Sūtra*, which described the state which he was now experiencing:

'In utter purity, the bright light pervades all,
With its shining stillness enfolding the great void.
Worldly things, when closely looked at,
Are but illusions seen in dreams.'

He also asked prefect Hu to prohibit the felling of trees on the mountains so that timber could be available for the building of new monasteries.

The following year, he thought of repaying his debt of gratitude to his parents and decided to write, with his own blood, a copy of the huge *Avataṁsaka Sūtra* for the purpose. He conversed with visitors and wrote simultaneously without making a single mistake. When asked how he could do so, his companion Miao Feng said: 'My friend is familiar with the state of Samādhi.'

As predicted by the Buddha in the sūtras, Han Shan also had many good dreams in which he saw master Ch'ing Liang, Maitreya and Mañjuśrī who gave him instruction, and in which he achieved the same stages as when he was awake. This shows that he was able to control his mind even in his sleep.

Now he turned his attention to the welfare of the imperial family so that peace and security prevailed all over the country. The empress mother asked him to pray for the birth of the heir to the throne whereas the emperor's second wife requested Taoist prayers so that she might become mother of the inheritor. In order not to be involved in court intrigue, he left the capital and settled at Lao Shan on the seashore. When the empress mother heard of his new place of abode, she donated three thousand gold pieces for rebuilding an ancient temple for him there, but he declined them and asked the court envoy to use the money for the relief of famine victims in the region. He converted people there to the Dharma.

ANOTHER MAJOR AWAKENING

In his fortieth year he found real rest in the new abode which enabled him to lay down all worldly activities and find an incomparable bliss. One evening, after a meditation, he realised another major awakening as described in *The Śūraṅgama Sūtra*:

> 'Your body and mind as well as external mountains,
> rivers, space and the great earth are but phenomena
> within the wondrous bright True Mind.'

This is the whole sūtra's field of insight, or what the Ts'ao Tung (Japanese, Soto) sect calls *Integration of the real and the seeming, prince and minister in harmony, host in host*, and *absolute achievement*.[1] For the benefit of his disciples, he immediately related his awakening in a manuscript entitled *The Hanging Mirror of the Śūraṅgama Sūtra*, which was later followed by a more comprehensive commentary on the same sūtra entitled *The Thorough Meaning of The Śūraṅgama Sūtra*.

HIS OTHER BODHISATTVA-WORKS

In his forty-eighth year, he gave all the temple's store of provisions to the victims of a severe famine in the region, and then sailed to Manchuria to purchase beans to relieve the suffering.

He had previously suggested that the empress mother reduce the court's daily expenses on food in order to save money for rebuilding Pao En monastery which was the aim of his visits to Peking, but

[1] Cf *Ch'an and Zen Teaching, Second Series*, p. 127. Rider, London.

those who opposed his suggestion found pretexts to sow discord between the emperor and his mother. Here his misfortune began. He was ordered to appear in court, was found guilty of building temples illegally and was banished to Lei Chou, a small town on the sea facing Hainan Island in south China.

In his fifty-first year, he arrived at Canton where a scholar asked him about the profound meaning of a sentence quoted from *The Book of Changes*: 'One can realise the truth only after understanding the condition of day and night.' Han Shan had not read the book but since he could now take up the *host* position at will, the answer was ready on his lips, and he replied: 'This is a Sage's indication to men that they should awaken to that which is beyond birth and death.' This shows that he could interpret correctly not only the Buddha Dharma but the doctrines of all other religions as well.

On arrival at Lei Chou, he began his commentary on *The Avataṁsaka Sūtra*. Because of a long drought, there was an extensive famine followed by an epidemic resulting in very many deaths. He and a scholar undertook to bury about ten thousand putrid corpses inside and outside the town. He then held a ceremonial service to pray for rain, and on the same day, heavy rain fell. From then on the epidemic was stamped out.

To a materialist and sceptic, this was pure coincidence, but to a Buddhist who has awakened to the Mind Dharma, there is nothing strange in what happened at Lei Chou. For since the mind creates our environment, the latter can be changed by an enlightened mind.

In his fifty-third year, he completed his commentary on *The Avataṁsaka Sūtra*. He then wrote his commentary on *The Lotus Sūtra* and a gāthā, *Purify Your Mind*, for a disciple. He devoted his time to other Bodhisattva-works of salvation. In his fifty-sixth year, he rebuilt the monastery of the Sixth Patriarch, and revived the Transmission of the Lamp which had been buried in oblivion for a very long time.

The master's best friend, Ta Kuan who was also an enlightened Ch'an monk, was the victim of a false accusation and was put in prison where he chanted the following gāthā before passing away:

'A smile comes not without a special cause.
Who knows that Nothingness contains no dust?
Henceforth I tuck up the feet my mother gave me;
The iron tree waits not for the spring to blossom.'

Han Shan wrote a biography of Ta Kuan.

In his sixty-first year, after the proclamation of an amnesty, the master was released and went to the monastery of the Sixth Patriarch. The following year he wrote a commentary on *The Tao Teh Ching*. He then went to the West River to buy timber to renovate the main hall of the monastery, and when he was accused of embezzling the funds by some degenerate monks, he read *The Diamond Sūtra* and then wrote *The Diamond Cutter of Doubts* which we have presented in *Ch'an and Zen Teaching, First Series* (Rider, London). He also wrote commentaries on other sūtras and śāstras.

In his sixty-ninth year he left the monastery of the Sixth Patriarch and went to Kuang Shan where he stayed. He was later invited to return to Ts'ao Ch'i, which he did in his seventy-seventh year. He passed away when seventy-eight.

A careful study of Han Shan's autobiography which follows in Part V of this volume will show that the master began his Ch'an training from the correct point of departure, with concentration of mind to wipe out all rising thoughts so as to realise singleness of thought which was later replaced by singleness of mind, that is the condition of dhyāna. In the third volume of our *Ch'an and Zen Teaching Series*, p. 44 (Rider, London), we mentioned three kinds of dhyāna, or states of mental stillness: the *worldly*, *supramundane* and *supreme*.

THE WORLDLY DHYĀNA

The master achieved the *worldly dhyāna* when, in his nineteenth year, he had visions of the Three Holy Ones of the Western Paradise; in his twentieth year, he did not notice a single person in the crowded market-place; and in his twenty-eighth year, he experienced the manifestation of the aggregate of form. All this only showed good progress in his Ch'an training but was still on the worldly plane.

From letters received from some of my readers abroad, I have found that they have also succeeded in realising the *worldly dhyāna* which shows excellent progress in their meditation. I would urge them to read now *The Sūtra of Complete Enlightenment* which I have presented in *Ch'an and Zen Teaching, Third Series*, and which they will certainly understand well because of their entry into the stream of meditation. However, students of Ch'an Buddhism should never be satisfied with this initial progress but should continue their training until they realise the *supramundane* and *supreme dhyāna*.

THE SUPRAMUNDANE DHYĀNA

In his twenty-ninth year, the master, after reading *The Chao Lun*, suddenly awakened to Sen Chao's expounding of the immutability of all phenomena, and all his doubts about coming and going disappeared. This was his first experience of *supramundane dhyāna*, and his companion Miao Feng congratulated him, saying: 'I am glad you now have some capital for staying on the mountain.' He achieved a major awakening in his thirtieth year when he successfully practised Avalokiteśvara's method of perfection by turning back the faculty of hearing to disengage it from the thunder of mountain torrents. One day while sitting on a bridge as usual, he felt as if his body vanished and the sound of the water was no more heard. Another day while standing he suddenly entered the state of Samādhi which he described in the following gāthā:

'When in a flash the mad mind halts, inner organs
And all outer objects are thoroughly perceived.
As the somersaulting body hits and shatters space,
The rise and fall of all things are viewed without concern.'

This is the *supramundane dhyāna* leading to the state of Samādhi which the master experienced after wiping out both time and space, and which later enabled him to converse with visitors while at the same time copying the huge *Avataṁsaka Sūtra* without making a single mistake.

THE SUPREME DHYĀNA

In his thirty-first year during a heavy snowfall, Han Shan and Ch'e K'ung sat in meditation in a hut at Dragon Gate and both entered the state of Samādhi. Later in the same hut, the master and Miao Feng sat in meditation during another heavy snowfall and had the same experience. The master succeeded in maintaining this state of *supreme dhyāna* even in dreams when he saw Ch'ing Liang, Maitreya and Mañjuśrī. In his forty-seventh year, he recorded: 'I had the most wonderful time of my life while with master Ta Kuan; both of us sat face to face for forty days and nights in the state of deep Samādhi.' This was his experience of *supreme dhyāna* which was indescribable. If a Ch'an master were asked about it, he would remain speechless as Vimalakīrti did at Vaiśālī, or would simply show his two hands wide open.

Practisers of the Mind Dharma should follow the example set by Han Shan and should never satisfy themselves with some little progress in the initial stage of meditation; they should always refrain from giving rise to pride, self-importance and contempt of others which can only hinder their quest of the Truth.

We have gradually presented some important technical terms of Mahāyāna and Ch'an Buddhism, which we have inherited from enlightened masters of the past, and which have not been invented by us. It is a matter for regret that a few book-reviewers who are not familiar with the Mahāyāna and Ch'an vocabulary have criticised certain technical terms which are beyond their reach. As we have written earlier, it is most important for us to bury pride and prejudice before we can practise meditation with a view to awakening to the *Host* position so that we can understand the full import of profound idioms which accord well with the various stages of spiritual advance. It is idle to pretend that we can dispense with meditation and use our intellect or monkey mind to interpret these stages which are totally unknown to us.

For instance, the idiom *voidness* or *the void* (K'ung) is used by the Buddha to wipe out the illusion of ego and things so that His disciples can awaken to the absolute state which is *empty* or *void* of all dualities, but He does not teach nihilism which is but heresy. When His disciples cling to the void, He speaks of the *voidness of the void* (K'ung K'ung) to eradicate their discrimination. When they again cling to the voidness of the void, he speaks of the Absolute That Is (Miao Yu).

The Buddhist term Ch'ing Ching Hsin, literally pure and clean heart or *pure and clean mind*, cannot be translated by 'unmixed mind' and 'mind without objects' as wrongly suggested by a book-reviewer, because a *pure and clean mind* is not only pure but also cannot be soiled or screened by ignorance, whereas an 'unmixed' crystal ball, although pure and devoid of foreign matter, becomes covered with mud when dropped on wet ground.

The Buddha speaks of space merely to give an idea of the all-embracing state of Dharmakāya, but a reviewer has wrongly insisted that space is the essential body of the Buddha. If Dharmakāya is *Space*, then which body is *Time*? In our practice of the Dharma, are we to revert later to Space and Time to continue our illusory existence in Saṃsāra?

We are disciples of the Buddha and deeply regret we cannot change the profound meanings intended by the ancients. For we do not want to be involved in the law of causality for defacing the Buddha-Dharma thereby causing untold harm to sincere students of Buddhism in the West who are as keen as ourselves to keep away from the realm of illusion and suffering.

All brackets in the following autobiography of Master Han Shan are mine and are added to make the original text more clear to readers.

C

PART V

The Autobiography
of Ch'an Master Han Shan
(1546-1623)

HAN SHAN TA SHIH NIEN P'U

From Master Han Shan's 'Journey in Dreamland'
Translated by Upāsaka Lu K'uan Yü (Charles Luk)

My first year (1546–7)
I was a native of Chuan Chiao, a district of Chin Ling [Nanking].
My surname was Tsai. My father's name was Yen Kao. My mother's
surname was Hung. All her life she worshipped Avalokiteśvara
Bodhisattva. One night in a dream, she saw the Bodhisattva leading
a boy by the hand and entering our house. My mother received the
boy and carried him in her arms. She became pregnant, and, when
I was born, my body was clothed in layers of white membrane that
resembled garments. My birth took place on the twelfth day of the
tenth month of that year [November 5, 1546].

My second year (1547–8)
On my birthday I became ill and was on the verge of breathing my
last. Mother prayed before the Bodhisattva and promised that if I
recovered she would permit me to leave home to join the Saṅgha.
She also registered my name at the Temple of Long Life. For this
reason I was given the name of H'u Shang [Buddhist Monk].

My third year (1548–9)
I used to sit alone and did not like to play. My grandfather would
say: 'This child is like a wooden stake.'

My seventh year (1552–3)
My uncle had a deep affection for me. My mother sent me to school.

One day my uncle died and his body was placed on a bed. When I returned my mother did not tell me the truth. She said: 'Uncle is sleeping; you can wake him up.' I called him a few times, and my aunt was painfully affected. 'Heavens!' she cried, 'where have you been?' I was very surprised and doubtful about what had happened. I asked mother: 'Uncle's body is here, where has he gone?' She replied: 'Uncle is dead.' I enquired: 'He is dead, but where has he gone?' A doubt about all this surged in my mind. Soon after this my second aunt gave birth to a boy and mother took me to see her. I saw the baby and asked mother: 'Where did this baby come from and how did he get into aunt's belly?' Mother patted my face and said: 'Silly boy! And you, where did you come from and how did you get into mother's belly?' A keen desire to be clear about all this arose in my mind, and from that time I was unable to drive away my doubt about birth and death.

My eighth year (1553-4)

Mother arranged for my schooling and board at a relative's house on the opposite side of the river and told me I could only come home once a month. One day after my visit, I was so hungry for my mother that I refused to leave her. She became angry, whipped me, and chased me to the river bank. When I refused to board the ferry-boat, she took me by the hair and threw me into the river. Then she went straight home without turning her head. My grandmother who saw all this called for help: I was rescued and brought home. Mother said: 'This boy has no talents. If he is not thrown into the river, what is the use of keeping him?' Again she whipped and chased me as if she did not want me. At that time I thought my mother was cruel; thereafter, I did not think of my home. [Because of her love for me] mother used to shed tears on the other side of the river. My grandmother scolded her [for being so harsh] but mother said: 'His affection must be cut off so that he can study seriously.'

My ninth year (1554-5)

I continued my studies in the school of a monastery where I heard the monks recite *The Sūtra of the Bodhisattva Avalokiteśvara* who can

save the world from suffering. I was delighted by it and asked a
monk to give me a copy of the sūtra which I managed to read and
recite. Mother worshipped Avalokiteśvara, and when she burned
incense and prostrated before him, I always followed her. One day
I told her: 'The Bodhisattva has a sūtra.' She replied: 'I didn't know.'
I then recited it and mother was very delighted. She said: 'Where
did you get it? Your voice is like that of an old monk.'

My tenth year (1555–6)

Mother was very strict when she made me do school work at home.
I was uneasy and asked her: 'What is the use of studying?' She said:
'To become an official.' I asked: 'Of what rank?' She replied: 'Any
one from the lowest up. And if one has talent, one can even become
a chief minister of State.' I asked: 'After reaching the rank of chief
minister of State, what then?' She replied: 'Retirement.' I then
said: 'After working so hard all one's life, isn't it a pity to stop
when one's reached the goal? Then what is the use? I want to do
something that doesn't stop.' She said: 'For you who have no
talents, all that remains is to become a wandering monk.' I asked:
'What is a wandering monk? Is it good to be one?' Mother said:
'Monks are disciples of Buddha and wander all over the country;
they are free and at ease and receive offerings everywhere.' I told
her: 'That suits me.' She said: 'I am only afraid that you won't be so
lucky.' I asked: 'Why does this require good luck?' She said: 'It is
easy to find academicians, but it is not easy to find people who leave
their homes to become Buddhas and Patriarchs.' I said: 'I am such a
lucky one, but I am afraid that you will not permit me to leave you.'
She said: 'If you have this kind of good luck, I can part with you.
But keep this between us.'

My eleventh year (1556–7)

One day I saw a few monks coming with gourds and bamboo hats
on their shoulders. I asked my mother: 'Who are they?' She replied:
'They are wandering monks.' I was delighted and watched them.
When they arrived they put their loads on the ground and leaned
against some trees. Then they asked for offerings. Mother told them:

'Venerable Sirs, please sit down.' She immediately prepared tea and a vegetarian meal which she reverently offered to them. After the meal the monks got to their feet, put the loads on their shoulders, and each of them raised a hand. Mother immediately fled, saying: 'Venerable Sirs, please do not give thanks.' The monks then departed. I said: 'Why were they so impolite? They didn't even thank us for the meal.' Mother said: 'There would be no merit if they gave thanks.' I said to myself: 'This is why these monks are so highly regarded.' And I did not stop thinking about all this. I wanted to be able to leave home but I was uneasy because I had not the means to do so.

My twelfth year (1557-8)

I was not interested in worldly things. My father wanted to find me a wife but I immediately prevented him from doing it. One day I learned from a monk who had come from the [southern] capital [Nanking] that abbot Hsi Lin of Pao En monastery had great virtues, so I wanted to go there and to follow him. I talked to my father who refused to let me go. I talked to my mother who told my father: 'We have raised him, and now we must allow him to follow his own inclination. Let him achieve his own goal.' I was then sent away and arrived at the monastery in the seventh month of the year. The abbot saw me and said with delight: 'This boy has an appearance which is not common, and it would be a pity if he were to become a vulgar monk.' At that time master Wu Chi began to give lectures in the Tripiṭaka Hall of the monastery. The abbot's old master took me to see him. Among those present was Chao Ta Chou who, seeing me, said with delight: 'This boy will be a teacher of men and devas.' He patted me asking: 'Would you like to become an official or a Buddha?' Immediately I replied: 'A Buddha.' Chao said: 'This boy should not be neglected; he should be suitably taught.' When I listened to the lecture—although I did not understand it well—I was [in the keen state of mind] of one who knew of something but could not reach it.

My fourteenth year (1559–60)
First the abbot's master selected from [the abbot's] disciples a monk
named Chun, who was of good education and character, to be my
teacher. The latter first taught me *The Lotus Sūtra* which, within
three months, I was able to recite by heart. I next studied other
currently recited sūtras which I also learned by heart. The abbot
said: 'This boy can be taught and should not be wrongly guided.'
A good teacher was then found for me.

My seventeenth year (1562–3)
The abbot's master asked my tutor to teach me literature for the
scholar's examinations. I began with *The Four Books* which I
studied simultaneously and then went on to *The Five Classics*,
The Sages' Books, history, ancient literature, poetical composition
and light verse which I could write immediately. My *'On the
River'* was highly appreciated by all the members of our literary
group. At that time I was often ill and wanted to abandon my
studies.

My nineteenth year (1564–5)
Because the members of our group were seeking worldly success,
I was advised to go to the capital for the scholar's examination. At
the time master Yun Ku, who had the Right Dharma Eye, was
staying on Ch'i Hsia Mountain, where my abbot supported and
visited him. On each visit he was induced to remain there for a
month. I diligently served them and often heard master Yun Ku's
teaching.

When master Yun Ku came from the mountain and learned that
I had been advised to sit for the scholar's examination, he became
apprehensive that I might leave the monastery. He encouraged me
to abandon all worldly things and to practise Ch'an in order to
realise the wonder of the mind. He enumerated the masters who had
transmitted the Lamp and told me the lives of the great monks,
advising me to read about them. In the bookcase I found *The Sayings
of Chung Feng*. I read it and before I had finished I was delighted. I
praised it and said: 'This is exactly what my mind likes.' Thereupon,

I decided to join the Sangha and requested my abbot's master to shave my head. I burned all my books and writings and concentrated on Ch'an training. Because I did not know its essentials, I concentrated my mind on repeating Amitābha Buddha's name. I did so for days and nights without interruption, and soon one night I saw in a dream Amitābha Buddha standing in space to the West. His radiant appearance was seen clearly; I knelt at his feet and my attachment to him was great. I hoped that I would see the two attendant Bodhisattvas, Avalokiteśvara and Mahāsthāmaprāpta, and immediately they appeared in half-size. From that time the Three Holy Ones of the Western Paradise appeared radiantly and constantly before my eyes. Consequently, I was confident that my practice would be successful.

That winter the Ch'an hall of the monastery was used as a ceremonial Dharma hall, and master Wu Chi was invited to lecture on *The Hua Yen Hsuen T'an* [a commentary on *The Avataṁsaka Sūtra* by State master Ch'ing Liang]. I went there to receive full ordination and remained to listen to him. When the lecturer came to the paragraph on the Samādhi of the Ocean Symbol[1] in 'The Chapter of the Ten Wonder Doors', I immediately awakened to the deep meaning of the unobstructed interpermeation and intermerging of all things in the Dharmadhātu.[2] I greatly admired State master Ch'ing Liang and consequently took the name of Cheng Yin.[3] I requested the lecturer to verify and confirm my understanding, and he said: 'Is it your inclination to enter that Dharma-door [to Enlightenment]?'

I understood that the Ch'ing Liang Mountain was so named because in winter it was covered with ice and in summer snow still lay on it, thus explaining the lack of the sun's heat. From that moment, whether I walked or stood still, the snowy and icy scenery of that site was visible before my eyes. I then vowed to go and live

---

[1] The vastness of meditation which reveals all phenomena as springing from the underlying Reality.

[2] The unifying and underlying spiritual Reality that is regarded as the ground or cause of all things; the absolute from which all things proceed.

[3] Clear Impression.

on the mountain. Nothing else would interest me as the idea of retiring from the world was constantly present in my mind.

My twentieth year (1565–6)
On the sixteenth day of the first month, the abbot passed away. On a New Year's Eve two years before his death, he had summoned all his disciples and told them: 'I am eighty-three years old and soon will leave. I have over eighty disciples, but none of them continues my sect.' He then tapped my back and said: 'I wish I could see him grown up, but it is too late now. In spite of his youth, he is already as able as a man. After my death he should be consulted for decisions about all matters, big or small, concerning this monastery. Do not slight him because of his youth.' This command was accepted by the sighing disciples. On the seventh day of the new year, he dressed himself and made a tour of the huts, bidding farewell to everyone and all were astounded. Three days later he gave instructions to be carried out after his death. He was slightly indisposed, and, when his disciples brought him medicine, he refused it, saying: 'I am leaving; what is the use of taking medicine?' All his disciples assembled to repeat Amitābha Buddha's name for five days and nights. Firmly holding his rosary close to his body in a dignified position, he died. Throughout his entire life the abbot had never ceased to recite *The Diamond Sūtra*. For thirty years he had been the abbot of Pao En monastery. Everyone was stunned when after his death, on the eighteenth day of the third month, the abbot's room caught fire.

In the tenth month of the same year, master Yun Ku organised a Ch'an meeting at Tien Chieh, assembling fifty-three well-known and virtuous persons for Ch'an meditation. The master urged me to attend. He was listened to by the young new abbot of the monastery, and I was able to attend the meeting.

When I began my Ch'an practice, I did not know how to control my mind and was not at ease. Holding an incense stick, I called on the master for instruction. He taught me to look into the Kung An, 'Who is repeating the Buddha's name?' Thus I held on to this single thought, and during the following three months, I, as if in a dream, did not notice the assembly's presence and had no idea of what was going on. Everyone believed that I had taken a great resolution. During the first few days, because of overstrain, an abscess appeared on my back; it was large, swollen and red. This worried the master. Putting on my robe, I went to pray before the shrine of Wei T'o [the spiritual guardian of the monastery]; I said: 'O Protector of the Dharma, this must be some karma of hatred from a previous life which is now claiming me, and the debt must be paid. I now vow to recite *The Avataṁsaka Sūtra* ten times and pray for a three month respite [from this karma of hatred] to enable me to complete the period set for Ch'an meditation. After that I will pay the debt.' After midnight I felt very tired and fell asleep on the meditation bed. I did not even know when the meditation ended. When I got up, I forgot about my abscess. At daybreak the master inquired about my ailment, and I replied: 'Master, I am all right.' When I was examined the abscess had already gone down; everyone was astounded. Thus I was able to complete the entire Ch'an period, and when I left my seat my mind was in exactly the same state as when I had been in meditation. I went to the crowded market place but did not see a single person. All the monks of the monastery were stunned.

The Ch'an sect from the day it first reached the eastern provinces south of the Yangtse River failed to prosper until the time of master Yun Ku. Nevertheless, I was the only monk practising Ch'an in the monastery. At that time monks wore lay clothing which was mostly of bright colours. I threw away all my garments and wore a Saṅgha robe; people found this strange when they saw me.

My twenty-first year (1566–7)

After the Ch'an meditation, on the twenty-eighth day of the second month, torrential rain fell. The stūpa was suddenly struck by lightning and the shrine caught fire; between five and seven that evening all the halls and painted corridors, numbering one hundred and forty, were reduced to ashes. The young abbot was in charge and when the news of the fire reached the emperor, an order was given to the department of justice to arrest him and eighteen senior monks.

All the other monks fled lest they too be involved. Since those who were left in charge did not know what to do, I went to try to save those who had been arrested; I carried salted vegetables for them to the jail which was some twenty [Chinese] miles away. I went there and returned to the monastery every day for three months without interruption. Aid was sought from all sides, thus saving their lives.

At that time Hsueh Lang, master Wu Chi's disciple who was a year older than me, was my dear friend; we were often taken for brothers. It was with him that I decided to rebuild the monastery. I said: 'This is an important affair, and if it is to materialise, we must have great virtue and wisdom. It is not an easy matter; you and I must take all the risks that are involved in practising the Dharma first and wait for the opportune time to execute our plan.' I then decided to make a long journey.

Soon the young abbot passed away, leaving no one to look after the community. When the old abbot had died, he had left no money; even his funeral expenses had been paid with borrowed funds. Therefore, there were outstanding debts, and if all the monks were not lodged there, this would mean the end of the community. Remembering the old abbot's instruction when he died (that I be consulted about decisions concerning the monastery), I made arrangements to pay all the debts. The balance of the money available was divided among the monks; the community was thus saved from dissolution.

That winter I followed master Wu Chi and listened to his talk on *The Lotus Sūtra* at Tien Chieh monastery. As I had decided to make a long journey, I searched for a monk to be my companion; but after a long wait, I could not find one. One day I noticed that the latrines were exceptionally clean and thought that the monk who looked after them must be an extraordinary man. When I went to see him I found he was a sick monk whose face was yellow and swollen and this increased my curiosity. Each morning when I got up, I found the latrines were already very clean; I did not know when the man did his chore. One night I purposely did not go to bed and went down the corridor to investigate. The place was already in good order when the monks left the meditation hall. A few days later it was not clean, and the monk was not to be seen. I asked the monk in charge who said that the sanitation man was ill and resting in the guest room. I went to see him and found him in an appalling condition. I asked him: 'Are you all right?' He replied: 'I already support my karmic body badly, and when it is sick, it becomes quite unbearable.' I asked: 'Why?' He said: 'When I see that the meal is ready, I regret I cannot remain indifferent to it.' I realised that he was a sincere man and brought him some cakes. When I asked his name, he said: 'Miao Feng, a native of Foochow.' I at once proposed that he accompany me on my journey. A few days later when I called on him again but did not find him, I realised that he did not like being disturbed by me and had departed secretly.

My twenty-second year (1567-8)
I arranged for master Yun Ku to become head of the monastery in order to save it from falling into ruins after the disastrous fire. Debts amounting to one thousand gold coins had been contracted through me which the monks could not pay, so I arranged to have them met within three years. The local authorities instructed the monastery to open a free school for the monks, and I was invited to be the teacher. There were two hundred pupils, so I had to work as a scholar again.

My twenty-third year (1568-9)
I left the school and taught at Kao Tso monastery. This was because of the conditions prevailing at the [damaged] monastery.

My twenty-fourth and twenty-fifth years (1569-71)
During these two years I taught at Chin Shan monastery's school.

My twenty-sixth year (1571-2)
I went to Lu Shan Mountain with my intimate friend Hsueh Lang. Upon reaching Nan K'ang, we heard that tigers were roaming about the place: we did not dare to climb the mountain. We took advantage of the favourable wind to go to Chi An. We visited Ch'ing Yuan and saw the monastery in ruins and monks who had

let their hair grow. I had an ardent desire to rebuild the monastery and told the local authorities about it. All monks under forty years old were selected; over forty of them had their heads shaved.

In the summer I returned from Ch'ing Yuan and arranged to put in order the work left by my master.

In the eleventh month of that winter, equipped with a rice bowl, I started my long journey. I was ready to leave for the north when Hsueh Lang tried to dissuade me, saying that I could not withstand the severe cold there and advising me to go to the south-eastern provinces where the scenery was very beautiful. I told him: 'We have the bad habit of living in soft, warm comfort and have to go where no comfort can be found in order to control our minds. As for a journey to the south-eastern provinces, it is just another commonplace.' With a bowl I started my journey.

My twenty-seventh year (1572–3)

I reached Yang Chou first and found my way barred by a heavy snowfall. I also became ill. After a long wait I went to the market place to beg for food but could not get any. Trying to guess the reason, I had a sudden idea and said to myself: 'I have two coins in my belt and can rely on them.' So I invited all the monks who were begging in vain for food in the snow to an eating house where with all my money I bought them a meal. The following day I went into the street and knocked at one or two doors. Now because I could speak audibly (which I could not do the day before), I was given food. I was delighted and said to myself: 'I am now strong enough to be heard above ten thousand [temple] bells.' Therefore, I named my bowl 'A utensil that can be heard above ten thousand bells'. I called my robe 'An implement that enables me to remain indifferent to the whole world' and composed the following poem in its honour:

> 'You confide a form to me,
> To you I entrust my mind.
> With you, my body nothing lacks,
> All things to me are trivial.
> Your long sleeves flow in the breeze, like

White clouds your mantle undulates.
You rise as on a wild swan's wings,
Easy as a swimming dragon.
Free am I in the universe to roam
Or on a wooden peak to stay or go.
Why wear garments [rare and] beautiful
When what matters is the frost and snow?'

In the seventh month of that year, I went to the [northern] capital [Peking] where I could not find a lodging. I begged for food and spent the whole day without getting any. Toward nightfall I went to a tea booth at Hsi Tai P'ing where I could only get a meal. I passed the night in I Chiao temple at H'o Ts'ao. The next day sub-prefect Wang Po Yu heard of my arrival and sent for me. Since his brother Wang Chung Yen was a member of a group [that had been formed at I Chiao temple], I was able to stay there for ten days. Afterwards I visited Dharma-master Maha Chung and followed him to Hsi Shan temple to listen to a talk on *The Miao Tsung Chao* [a commentary on the *Sūtra of the Meditation of Amitābha Buddha* according to the T'ien T'ai School]. On this occasion I composed a poem in remembrance of my intimate friend Hsueh Lang. After the talk the master detained me there to pass the winter and listen to lectures on *The Lotus Sūtra* and *Vijñāna-Mātra*. I asked the master to enlighten me on the doctrine of the three members of a syllogism [pratijñā, the proposition; hetu, the reason; and udāharaṇa, the example].

In the eleventh month Miao Feng arrived and called on me. His hair and beard were long, and he was wearing coarse clothing. First he announced himself as a salt merchant who wanted to see me. When he entered he asked: 'Do you recognise me?' I looked at him and saw his eyes. Suddenly I remembered the sanitary monk at Tien Chieh monastery and said: 'I do recognise you.' He said: 'Just a transformation.' I replied: 'But your fundamental face has not changed.' We both laughed but had no time to talk to each other. I inquired about where he was staying and learned he was at Lung Hua temple. I saw him again the following day; during the evening as we sat together I asked the reason for his strange appearance. He answered: 'I have stayed on the mountain for a long time; my hair has grown long and I have had no time to shave my head. As His Highness Prince Shan Yin has given a donation towards rebuilding a temple and ordered me here to collect *The Tripiṭaka* for it, I have come.' In reply to his question, I told him: 'I came here to search for you and to see the capital where I hope to find learned masters so that with their guidance I can stop my false thoughts.' He said: 'After our parting I always thought of you, and I was afraid that we would not meet again. Now that you have come, I will gladly accompany you when you go out begging for food and will guard you from the dogs.' We talked all night and at daybreak we parted with a smile.

I then called on master Pien Yung, and, after paying obeisance, I prayed him to show me the way in Ch'an practice. He did not reply, but only looked at me. I called on master Hsiao Yen who asked me where I came from. I said: 'From the South.' He asked: 'Do you remember the road that led you here?' I replied: 'Once trodden, it vanished.' He said: 'You are clear about the point of departure.'[1] I paid obeisance to him, stood at his side, and prayed for his instruction. He said a few words about the transcendental doctrine.

Commentary by disciple Fu Cheng

Dharma-master I Yu said: 'Ancestor Han Shan decided to make a long journey to the North, but Hsueh Lang tried to dissuade him. Han Shan purposely sent him to the town and leaving unnoticed braved the heavy snowfall. When Hsueh Lang returned to the monastery, he learned of his friend's departure and wept bitterly. And so master Han Shan composed a poem in remembrance of Hsueh Lang.'

My twenty-eighth year (1573–4)
In the first month, I went to the Five Peak Mountain [Wu T'ai

[1] i.e. the mind which should not abide anywhere.

Shan]. I bought a copy of *The Life Story of Ch'ing Liang* and visited the famous holy sites mentioned therein. When I reached the North Peak, I felt drawn by the fine story of Han Shan Mountain [lit. Silly Mountain] and asked a monk where it was. He pointed it out to me. I liked its strange beauty and took my second name after it. On this occasion I composed a poem which contained these lines:

'This Silly Mountain does not follow worldlings as they move,
  Should it not then be copied to halt my wandering mind?'

Because I could not endure the bitter cold in the midst of snow and ice, I did not stay there but returned to the capital. From there I went eastwards and begged for food. Reaching Chien Hisang Feng [Thousand Statue Peak], I saw a monk who was silent and of whom I also asked no questions. I stayed with him, picking up firewood and carrying water for both of us. I begged for my food and thus passed the summer. Subprefect Wang sent for me with a letter saying among other things: 'I fear you will starve in the eastern suburb.' In autumn I had to return because Ou Chen Pai of Ling Nan [Kwangtung], now one of the state's learned scholars whom I had not seen and with whom I had not exchanged letters for a few years, wished to see me as soon as possible.

Commentary by disciple Fu Cheng

I have read *The Annals of the Famous Mountains* where it is written: 'There was at Lung Men [The Dragon Gate] of the Five Peak Mountain a mountain which, according to legend, emperor Ch'in Shih Huang whipped but failed to move although once, by whipping a rock, he had succeeded in transforming it into a bridge that enabled him to cross the ocean in his quest for immortality. That is why the mountain was called Han Shan [or Silly Mountain].'

The story about the silent monk was related in detail by the Venerable Chuan in his Records:

'Master Han Shan met Miao Feng in the capital and they both decided to go together to the Five Peak Mountain, where they hoped to stay for their meditation. At that time Miao Feng was waiting for the delivery of *The Tripiṭaka* which had been ordered by prince Shan Yin but was not ready for the long journey. Master Han Shan stayed at Subprefect Wang Nan Ming's private studio.

'After a long wait master Han Shan one day wandered to P'an Shan Mountain and climbed until he reached its peak. By the side of the peak, a hermit lived in a stone cave. His head was grey and his face was of the colour of earth. Master Han Shan saluted him, but the hermit did not respond and remained silent. Master Han Shan knew that he was no ordinary man and sat down near him. After a while the hermit made some tea, took a cup, poured the tea and drank it. Master Han Shan also took a cup, poured some tea and drank it. After tea the hermit put the cup back and continued his meditation as before. Master Han Shan did the same. Later the hermit cooked rice; and when it was ready, he put it before his seat, took a bowl and chopsticks and ate. Master Han Shan also took a bowl and chopsticks and ate. After the meal the hermit sat as before; master Han Shan did the same. At night the hermit went for a walk; master Han Shan followed him but went in the opposite direction. The next day at tea time, master Han Shan boiled tea; and at meal time he cooked rice. The hermit drank tea and ate rice with him, and at night they both went out and walked as they had done the previous night. This continued for seven days. Then the hermit began to ask: "Virtuous One, where do you come from?" Master Han Shan replied: "From the South." The hermit asked: "Why did you come here?" Master Han Shan replied: "To seek you, the hermit." The latter said: "The hermit's face is like *this* and has nothing peculiar." Master Han Shan said: "The first day as I entered this cave, I immediately un-covered the hermit." The hermit smiled and said: "For over thirty years I have lived in this cave, and I only now have met one of my line." He invited master Han Shan to stay with him, and the guest forgot about his return.

'One night master Han Shan went out and walked as usual. Suddenly his forehead burst with a noise like thunder; everything

—including mountains, rivers, the earth, his body, mind and the universe [itself]—disappeared entirely. That voidness was not comparable to ordinary empty space; this state of still voidness lasted about the time it would take five [Chinese] inches of incense stick to burn. Gradually he felt the presence of his body and mind and the firm stance of his feet on solid ground. Opening his eyes he gradually saw again the mountains, rivers and the earth; everything that had surrounded him previously returned to normal. His body and mind became light and joyful, and the effect of all this was indescribable. He moved his feet to walk and felt that they were as light as air. When he returned to the cave, the hermit asked: "Why did your stroll last so long tonight?" Master Han Shan told him about what had just happened, and the hermit said: "This is only the [manifestation of] the aggregate of form [rūpa] and is not your real nature. I have been here for over thirty years, and, except when the wind blew or it rained or snowed, I have had the same experience every night while walking. If one does not allow oneself to be attracted by it, it will not obscure one's fundamental nature." Master Han Shan accepted the hermit's teaching and bowed his thanks.

'Master Han Shan stayed at the cave for a long time. When the whole collection of *The Tripiṭaka* was delivered [to Miao Feng in the capital] and he was ready for the return journey [to Prince Shan Yin at Ho Tung], he called on subprefect Wang and inquired about Master Han Shan's whereabouts. Subprefect Wang sent to P'an Shan Mountain to locate the master. The messenger heard that he was in the cave, came to see him, and informed him that the subprefect and Miao Feng were awaiting his return. Master Han Shan took leave of the hermit, but so great was his attachment to his host that it was difficult for him to go. However, there was an engagement to keep, and the hermit, with tears trickling down like pearls, accompanied Han Shan to the half-way point of the mountain path where he turned back.

'Upon his return to the capital, master Han Shan was welcomed by Miaro Feng and the subprefect. Smiling, they both said: "Why so late?" Master Han Shan told them about his experience during his stay at the cave. The subprefect said: "As it is, your stay on the mountain is over." Master Han Shan said: "That was only the roadside." He and Miao Feng looked at each other and laughed heartily.'[1]

During his lifetime the master's experiences, such as the one related above by the Venerable Chuan in a chapter of about six hundred Chinese characters in his *P'an Shan Records*, were too numerous for telling either orally or in writing; but in his autobiography the master recorded them in a few short sentences: The peak of a Thousand Statues, the silent monk, picking up firewood, carrying water and begging food in the summer. For him these experiences were just as familiar as his daily teas and meals. In spite of his attachment to the cave, he could leave it at will. Although his previous engagement was the direct cause of his departure, he also did not want to become a man of the Small Vehicle who sought only his own Enlightenment.

My twenty-ninth year (1574-5)

In the spring I visited the capital's Western Hill [Hsi Shan]. Gathering in the capital were the present generation's eminent scholars, such men as the two brothers Wang Feng Chou and Wang Lin Chou, the two brothers Wang Po Yu and Wang Chung Yen, and Ou Chen Pai of Ling Nan, who previously had enjoyed my esteem.

One day I visited Wang Feng Chou. Because I was young he believed he could handle me easily. With pride I acted as his guest and treated him as my host. As he was unwary and attempted to teach me poetry, I stared at him and left him without a word. He was not pleased and told his younger brother, Wang Lin Chou, about the incident. The next day, Wang Lin Chou came to see me. He said: 'Last night my elder brother lost an Eye.' I asked him:

[1] 'Your stay on the mountain is over' means 'Your training is completed and you have realised Enlightenment.' 'That was only the roadside' means 'I am still on the side of the Path, have not entered it and still require Ch'an training.'

'Have you that Eye?' He bowed and said: 'Now I have met you.'
Both of us laughed heartily.[1]

Returning to his elder brother, Wang Lin Chou said: 'Brother,
you have been defeated by a [modern] Vimalakīrti.'[2] So he wrote
and sent me a poem containing these two lines:

'Wang I was young and famous but in logic
He was no match for the old master Chih Tun.'

One day when I was staying with Wang Chung Yen, he saw me
reading a volume of The Tso Chuan and told me: 'Your natural
gift is powerful, and you have an inclination for literature. My elder
brother is an authority on contemporary literature. Why don't you
take up a [literary] career and make a name for yourself?' I laughed,
spat and said: 'I am waiting for the time when I will receive your
elder brother on his knees as he solicits this old monk's teaching on
the reason for the coming from the West.'[3] The young Wang was
displeased and reported all this upon his return to the subprefect who
said: 'Is it true? I see the Venerable Cheng Yin[4] has the essence of
the Tao in his bones and will certainly enter the Houses of Ta Hui
and Chung Feng.[5] He will certainly disdain such a trifle as literature,
but I am afraid his wanderings will hinder him.' One day reading a
poem that I had written on a paper fan and had given to his younger
brother, he noticed the following lines:

'Time and space are a cicada's wings
And the universe a horse's hair.'

[1] 'Eye' means the mind's Eye which can see through all phenomena to realise
the Truth. 'Now I have met you' means my mind's Eye has seen yours and we
have understood each other perfectly. Wang's brother, though unenlightened,
said all this in joke.
[2] Vimalakīrti was a native of Vaiśālī and assisted the Buddha in teaching the
Dharma.
[3] Bodhidharma's object when he came to China.
[4] Another name which Han Shan used when he was young.
[5] Ta Hui (lit. Great Wisdom) is a posthumous name conferred by the emperor
upon Ch'an master Fu Ji of Ching Shan Mountain at Hangchow; he died at
the age of 75 (A.D. 1163). Chung Feng was a Ch'an master of T'ien Mu Shan
Mountain in the Yuan dynasty; he died at the age of 61 (A.D. 1282).

He showed them to his younger brother, saying: 'Is that the writing of a literary monk?'[1]

Another day the subprefect invited Miao Feng and me to a vegetarian meal during which he told me: 'The decline of the Ch'an Sect is causing anxiety and I am not happy about it. From your bearing, one can sense your future success. But what is the use of wandering about the way you do?' I answered: 'The poor monk's[2] first motive is the great affair.[3] Consequently, I am travelling in order to call on enlightened persons; I will meet those of the present generation to receive their instructions so that I can arrest disturbing thoughts in the future. I am not a wanderer and yet I am leaving even now.' He said: 'That is true, but I have in mind no one who can be your teacher, and without Miao Feng you will have no friend.' I replied: 'In the past I selected him from among the assembly, and both of us agreed to be companions in our Ch'an practice. That is why we have come here to find each other, and we have met unexpectedly.' He said: 'This is wonderful. If both of you travel together, I will be glad to help you with money.'

By this time Miao Feng had received *The Tripiṭaka*. The prefect sent him two passes[4] and also wrote and sent me a literary composition on the occasion. One day he invited me to come quickly and said: 'Miao Feng is leaving. Why don't you hurry to see him off?' I replied: 'Oh, there is no need to hurry.' He said: 'I know you do not want to follow in other people's footsteps, but this [pride] is not always right; even the ancients did not blush about small things but were only ashamed of their fame being unknown everywhere. I only hope that you will do illustrious deeds for the Dharma. But why be at odds over a small matter?' I was moved and thanked him.

I then went immediately and saw Miao Feng who was already in

[1] In China there are monks who, instead of practising the Dharma, spend their time writing literary compositions and poems.

[2] A term used by monks in place of the personal pronoun 'I'.

[3] Self-enlightenment and enlightenment of others.

[4] Passes were issued to enable Miao Feng to obtain labour and new carts at the exchange point outside the capital. Men and carts hired in the capital would turn round at the exchange point and return to the capital. Passes were given to local authorities so that Miao Feng could hire new men and carts.

a cart with his pack. Seeing me he asked: 'Are you going too?' I
replied: 'I am ready' and climbed into the cart. This is why I left
without saying farewell to my friends.

That autumn in the eighth month, I crossed Men Chin rivulet and
reached the place where king Wu Wang reviewed the troops [prior
to his attack on the Shang state]. On this occasion I composed the
following verses to console the dead:

> 'A lone rock and one stone tablet on the river bank
> Are all that remains of where princes and nobles met.
> The emperor's rule, to last as long as heaven and earth,
> Should be as unceasing as the Yellow River's flow.'

I passed through the site where the two brothers, Pai I and Shu
Ch'i, had barred the passage of king Wu Wang's cavalry and without success had advised him not to attack the Shang state. I composed the following verses to console them:

> 'Of the deep thoughts some had when leaving fame and father-
> land behind,
> There only stay in mind an ancient temple, and a tall cypress.
> The Shou Yang Mountain, of such beauty, still reflects
> The mind which once tried to bar the horsemen's passage.'[1]

Next I visited Shao Lin monastery where the First Patriarch
[Bodhidharma] stayed; master Ta Chien Jun Tsung had just moved
in, so I called on but did not find him. I then left the mountain and
visited the ancient citadel of Lo Yang, the Sūtra-burning terrace and
the temple of the White Horse. After that, I overtook Miao Feng,
and in the ninth month reached Ho Tung and met prince Shan Yin
with whom I stayed for the winter.

At that time prefect Ch'en, Miao Feng and I were industrious in
our studies. We undertook the carving of wooden blocks for printing *The Chao Lun*[2] with explanatory notes. Until then I had not

[1] Both this and the previous poem illustrate the impermanence of the
phenomenal.

[2] A treatise by the famous Dharma-master Seng Chao, who was Kumārajīva's
disciple and assisted him in the translation into Chinese of sūtras brought from
India.

been very clear about the doctrine of the immutability of all things and the whirlwind that will destroy mount Sumeru. For a long time I had been in doubt about that doctrine; now as I read the text, I could not grasp the meaning. Then I came to the chapter on a Brahmin adept who left home in his youth and returned when his hair was white. A neighbour saw him and said: 'That man who used to live here still lives!' The Brahmin interjected: 'I look like but am no longer that man.' As one coming suddenly out of darkness, I perceived the full meaning of the doctrine and said: 'Now I can believe that fundamentally all things neither come nor go.' I got up from my meditation bed, prostrated myself before the Buddha shrine and did not have the perception of anything in motion. I lifted the blind and stood in front of the stone steps. Suddenly the wind blew through the trees in the courtyard, and the air was filled with flying leaves which, however, looked motionless. I said to myself: 'This is the whirlwind that will destroy Mount Sumeru and which is permanently still.' When I went to the back yard to make water, the urine seemed not to be running. I said: 'That is why the river pours but does not flow.' Thereafter, all my doubts about birth and death vanished; I composed the following verses:

> 'Of birth and death, day and night,
> Of running water, fading
> Flower, only now I know they are
> Because my nostrils downwards face.'[1]

The next day Miao Feng saw me and said joyfully: 'What have you got?' I replied: 'Last night I saw on the river bank two iron oxen struggling to enter the water and up to now no news from them.'[2] Miao Feng said laughingly: 'I am glad you now have some capital for living on the mountain.'

Shortly afterwards prince Shan Yin invited Ch'an master Fa

[1] A Ch'an term meaning 'From root to branches', i.e. the changing phenomenal come from the unchanging root or self-nature; birth and death, etc., are just creations of mind which wanders outside.

[2] 'Two iron oxen' stand for body and mind which vanish completely; the elimination of concepts of duality.

Kuan to come. Long ago I had esteemed the master highly, and when I saw him I was glad to be able to hear his teaching. I talked to him and found that our opinions did not differ. I asked for his instruction, and he told me: 'Your practice should be outside mind, intellect and consciousness; and your study should go beyond the saintly and the worldly.' I gained a deep understanding of his instruction. When he talked his voice was like the sound of a heavenly drum; I understood that when a man has realised his mind, his talking and breathing are really different [from those of the vulgar]. I had a great respect for him.

One day he picked up a poem of mine and read it. He said: 'How do you get these beautiful verses?' Then he laughed and said: 'Yes, they are beautiful, but that other passage is still not open.'[1] I asked: 'Is your other passage open?' He replied: 'I spent thirty years seizing dragons and catching tigers; today I let a rabbit escape from the grass and come out to jump.' I said: 'Venerable Sir, you are not a man who can seize dragons and catch tigers.' He took his staff and intended to strike me, but I held it with one hand and with the other pulled his beard, saying: 'You talk of a [big] rabbit but it is just a [small] toad.' He smiled and withdrew.[2]

Another day he told me: 'You don't need to go anywhere else. I hope that both of us will spend our old age together at Fu Niu.' I said: 'I see that your knowledge of the Buddha-Dharma and your power of speech are equal to those of [the eminent master] Ta Hui, but your attitude has shown mental disorder all day. Why do you hum, talk and gesticulate all day?' He replied: 'That is my Ch'an sickness. When I achieved my first awakening, words and sentences came to me in endless succession day and night and could not be stopped. This became my Ch'an sickness.' I asked: 'When this illness starts, how is it cured?' He replied: 'When it begins, if one cannot see into its unreality, one must have a learned master to beat one soundly enough so that one falls into a deep sleep. Then the sickness

[1] 'The other passage' is the mind's Eye.
[2] Fa Kuang smiled to reveal *function* and withdrew to return it to *substance*. For detailed explanation of Substance and Function, cf *Ch'an and Zen Teaching, Second Series*. Rider, London.

will be gone when one awakens. I regret that I did not have such a stern hand [to beat me at the time].'

He knew that I was leaving for Five Peak Mountain in the first month of the following year and wrote a poem for me that contained these two lines:

'For clear vision ride a lion high up in the clouds,
But the dragon in the cave should be set free to rest.'[1]

He asked me: 'Do you know this?' I replied: 'I do not.' He said: 'I don't want you to catch a dead snake.'[2]

For a very long time, our Ch'an sect had no learned masters, but after meeting master Fa Kuang I realised there were some who were very experienced teachers.

Prince Shan Yin heard that my parents were still living and offered me two hundred gold pieces for their remaining years. I declined them and said: 'This poor monk is just beginning his journey and is still unable to save himself. How can he involve his parents in this?' I was successful in having the prince grant my request to give the money to master Fa Kuang.

My thirtieth year (1575–6)

In the first month Miao Feng and I left Ho Tung and went to Five Peak Mountain. On the way we passed through P'ing Yang, Miao Feng's hometown. When he was young, his parents had died during a severe famine and since he was poor they had been buried without coffins. Now with money donated by prince Shan Yin and one or two other officials, I selected a high, dry site for a common grave and wrote an inscription for the tombstone. Miao Feng's lay surname was Hsu and he had lived in the eastern suburbs of P'ing Yang. He was a descendant of Hsu Ch'u of the times of *The Spring and Autumn Annals*.

[1] If you want to awaken to Reality, you should practise the transcendental Ch'an, but the first thing is to set your inner mind at rest as the point of departure.
[2] I want you to hit the *first rate meaning* but not the *third* one. (Cf *Ch'an and Zen Teaching, Second Series*, p. 93. Rider, London.)

Now prefect Hu Shun An heard of my arrival and stay outside the town, but he could not meet me. Since I was ready to continue my journey, he sent me travel passes.[1] I said: 'I am journeying and already have straw sandals which are quite enough for me. I do not need passes.' As I was on foot he overtook me at Ling Shih. We went to the town and stayed there for a few days. Messengers were sent to accompany me to Five Peak Mountain.

On the fifth day of the second month, we reached and stayed at T'a Yuan temple. Its abbot, master Ta Fang, selected the Dragon Gate of the North Peak for my stay. It was indeed the most retired and lofty site there. On the third day of the third month, I found beneath a snowdrift a few old huts which I used for a dwelling place after the snow that hid them had been removed. All the mountains were covered with snow and ice, and the scenery was just like the vision which I had had previously[2] and which I had loved so much. My body and mind were taken by surprise as if I were entering the Paradise of Bliss. Soon after this Miao Feng left to visit Yeh Tai, and I was alone to live in the place. I concentrated my attention on a single thought, and, if a visitor came, I did not speak but only looked at him. After a long while, when a visitor came he resembled a tree stump. This state of mind continued until I had no idea about the meaning of a single [Chinese] character. At first a roaring gale blew frequently and when the thaw set in torrents of water rolled down the mountains and made a thunderous noise. In the stillness it was like that of a thousand marching troops and ten thousand horses galloping at full speed; it was very disturbing. When asked [earlier before he departed], Miao Feng had said: 'This surrounding is created by the mind and does not come from outside. The ancients said: "Whoever hears the sound of water without using the sixth consciousness for thirty years, will achieve Bodhisattva Avalokiteśvara's all-pervading wisdom."' Consequently I went to a wooden bridge where I sat every day. At first the noise of the water was audible as before. After a long while it could only be heard when

[1] The passes would have authorised Han Shan to hire carts and men for his trip. He chose to walk.
[2] See 1564-5, fourth paragraph.

thoughts surged in my mind and not when they ceased to rise. Suddenly one day while sitting on the bridge as usual, I felt as if my body did not exist and the sound of the water was not heard any more. Henceforth, all the sound and noise vanished completely; I was no longer disturbed by them.

My daily meals consisted of rye with wild vegetable and porridge. At the beginning of my stay, people gave me ten pints of rice; after six months some was still left.

One day after taking rice porridge, I went for a walk as usual and suddenly while standing entered the state of Samādhi. I did not feel the existence of my body and mind. There was only a great brightness, round and full, clear and still like a huge round mirror. All the mountains, rivers and the great earth appeared therein. When I recovered consciousness, I could not find my body and mind in the brightness; I composed these verses:

'When in a flash the mad mind halts, inner organs
And all outer objects are thoroughly perceived.
As the somersaulting body hits and shatters space,
The rise and fall of all things are viewed without concern.'

Thereafter, there was a still serenity within and without my body; no hindrance was met from any sounds or forms. Just then all my former doubts disappeared. When I looked at the rice cooker, it was already covered with dust. Because I was alone, I did not have any way of knowing how long I had been in the state of Samādhi.

In the summer Hsueh Lang came to the North to visit me. After his arrival at Five Peak Mountain, he could not help feeling, while we sat together in the hut, the loneliness and desolation of that miserable site; he left after spending two nights. In the winter I built myself a wooden hut.

Commentary by disciple Fu Cheng

When I was in the Tsung Ching hall of Chin Tzu temple, I heard the following story told by master Han Shan's three senior disciples Chih Wei, Hsu Chung and Hsin Lu:

'The master and his companion Miao Feng were at Dragon Gate on Five Peak Mountain. They used to sit on Lung Fan rock [The Rock of the Somersaulting Dragon] and listen to the bubbling spring. Throughout the year the sound of the spring was continuous. If it was not heard, entry into the state of Samādhi became possible. As Miao Feng realised that the master was about to enter that state, he left for another place. The master entered that state but did not know for how long when it was over. The only indication was the thick layer of dust that covered the rice cooker.

'From the above we can see that without having achieved awakening [Chinese, Wu; Japanese, Satori], one cannot enter Samādhi; and that without austere training, one cannot achieve an awakening. The ancients said: "There are eighteen major awakenings and numberless minor ones." People who say now that there is only one awakening are wrong.'

The life story of Dharma-master Hsueh Lang relates:

'That day Hsueh Lang was looking for master Han Shan and passed through Sung Shao and Fu Niu before reaching Dragon Gate on Five Peak Mountain where he found the master beneath a heap of ice and snow. Hsueh Lang wore round his waist a small bag of hot rice against the bitter cold and swore he would keep company with the master either dead or alive. Master Han Shan told him: "Each of us has his own inclination according to his causal affinity. Yours is to carry on the Dharma so that it can continue to live forever. Therefore, it is not advisable for you to spend your life in this dry and lonely place. In the Chiang Nan region, the Dharma is now buried in oblivion. You should continue the work left by our master Wu Chi and carry out his will in order to be the Eye of men and devas and to fulfil the purpose of your leaving home."

'Hsueh Lang agreed and left after an earnest talk with the master. Later he became a Dharma-master in various districts of the San Wu area where he taught the Dharma for thirty years. He was surrounded by a large number of followers and was very successful in spreading the Dharma.'

My thirty-first year (1576–7)

After my great awakening, having no one to confirm and testify it, I opened *The Śūraṅgama Sūtra* to verify my experience. I had not listened previously to lectures on this sūtra and so did not know its meaning. Now by using the power of the direct reasoning of the non-discriminating mind and without even the slightest use of its consciousness since there was no room for thinking, I gained after eight months complete comprehension of its profound meaning without having a single doubt left.

That spring in the third month, master Lien Chih visited Five Peak Mountain. He called on me and stayed for ten days. Our nightly talks proved that we were of like mind.[1]

In the seventh month of that autumn, prefect Hu of P'ing Yang, who had been transferred to the military administration at Yen P'ing, came to see me on the mountain. In the hut we ate only oats mixed with wild vegetables and leeks. At that time on the plain below, the weather was very hot. The prefect's men went to the frozen mountain stream to break up ice and chew it. Seeing this he said: 'This is another world. On our arrival here all our vulgar thoughts have been frozen too.'

That winter in the tenth month, master Ta Fang, abbot of T'a Yuan temple, was the victim of a false accusation and was brought before the court. He was found guilty and was sentenced to leave the Saṅgha and return to lay life. The monastery was thus threatened with ruin. At the time master Ch'e K'ung of Lu Shan came and stayed with me. Hearing of the court's decision he was pained. I said: 'There is no harm' and braved a heavy snowfall to visit prefect Hu [and ask him to release master Ta Fang]. Seeing me he said gladly: 'I have been thinking of the heavy snowfall on the mountain and have written you a letter which I intended sending by messenger with instruction to bring you down. I am glad you have come.' He then ordered the release of the abbot and the monastery was saved.

The prefect kept me for the winter at his headquarters, and

[1] Lien Chih was an enlightened Ch'an master but taught the Pure Land teaching which is suitable for all categories of men.

questioned me day and night on the Dharma of which I gave him an introductory sketch.

At that time viceroy Kao, who had been transferred to Ta Chun, heard that I was staying at the prefect's headquarters and told him: 'My residence has garden bowers graced with tablets bearing inscriptions of verse, and I would like a poem composed by an eminent person.' Prefect Hu promised that he would get one for the viceroy and told me about it. I said: 'I have not even a single [Chinese] character in my head. How can I compose a poem now?' I firmly refused and, as the viceroy insisted repeatedly on having one from me, the prefect was compelled to renew his request. Finally I put a collection of ancient and modern poetry on a sidetable to stimulate my thinking. As soon as I opened a volume at random and began to think, words and sentences came to me so rapidly with the thinking process in motion that they could not be stopped. When prefect Hu, who had left me a short time before, returned to the studio, I had already written twenty to thirty poems. Immediately I realised what had happened and said to myself: 'This is the demon of literary habits.' I paused and gave one poem to him to satisfy his desire. I did not dare show him the others; but the thinking process could not be stopped! Imperceptibly, all the literary prose, poems and verses which I had read or written before appeared in front of me and crowded and filled space. They could not have been ejected even if my body had been nothing but open mouths. I did not even know what my body and mind were. I pondered closely over all this and felt as if my body were about to rise. I had no alternative but to let things take their course.

The following day when the viceroy left, prefect Hu escorted him, and I was left alone. I thought of my experience and said to myself: 'This is exactly the Ch'an sickness that master Fa Kuang told me about. Now I have caught it, and who can cure it? What I can do now is to sleep and if it is deep I will be lucky.' I then closed the door and tried to sleep. At first I could not, but a long while later I felt as if I were sleeping while seated. A boy servant knocked at the door and pushed it but received no answer. When prefect Hu returned, he learned of this and ordered that the window be broken for the studio to be entered. I was seated, wrapped in my robe. He called me but I did not answer. He shook me but I did not move.

There was a Buddha shrine in the studio, and there was a small musical instrument called a ch'ing on the table. [One day previous to this deep sleep] prefect Hu had picked up that instrument and asked me: 'What is it and what is its use?' I had told him: 'In the West [i.e. India] when a monk enters the state of Samādhi and cannot waken from it, this instrument is used to awaken him.' Prefect Hu suddenly remembered what I had told him and now said: 'Venerable Master, are you in the state of Samādhi?' He took the instrument, and, holding it close to my ear, struck it a few tens of times. I was slowly and gradually awakened. When I opened my eyes, I did not know where I was. The prefect said: 'Immediately after I left, you shut the door, and this is the fifth day. What have you been doing?' I replied: 'I do not know, and this is my first breath.'

After saying this I sat silent and reflected carefully, but I failed to realise where I was and from where I had come. I looked back to my stay on the mountain and my past journeys and all those events were like things seen in a dream; after searching, not a thing could be found [in my now stilled mind]. All that previously had been in tumult in the great void was now as [still as] when the rains have passed and all the clouds dispersed. The air seemed thoroughly cleansed and everything was perfectly tranquil without a single appearance of shadows or images. The mind was empty and the surrounding objects were still; the resultant bliss was without compare. I said to myself:

'In utter purity, the bright light pervades all,
With its shining stillness enfolding the great void.
Worldly things, when closely looked at,
Are but illusions seen in dreams.'[1]

Those words spoken by the Buddha are true and not deceitful.'

As I decided to return to the mountain in the first month of the

[1] Quotation from Mañjuśrī's gāthā in *The Śūraṅgama Sūtra*. Cf *The Secrets of Chinese Meditation* and *The Śūraṅgama Sūtra*. Rider, London.

following year, I told prefect Hu: 'If unscrupulous traders are permitted to cut down the trees in the Five Peak Mountain forest, the holy sites of the Bodhisattvas will have no more timber.' He then wrote a petition requesting the prohibition of the felling of trees. The building of monasteries was thus made possible, this prohibition making timber available for that purpose.

Commentary by disciple Fu Cheng

The Venerable Chuan's Records relate:

'That year there was a heavy snowfall which lasted ten days so that all the peaks were covered with snow. The hut at Dragon Gate was hidden beneath more than one hundred [Chinese] feet of snow. Masters Han Shan and Ch'e K'un closed the doors and sat in meditation. Every day they poked the fire once to boil tea and cook rice. The monks and those who lived on the North and Central peaks and at the temple of the White Horse, numbering from two to three hundred, came down with hoes, baskets, brooms and exploring poles to try and find the path leading to Dragon Gate. As they explored, they dug; they came and went bravely and, after two days of searching, reached the hut. They shouted with joy, entered and said: "With all this on the mountain, it is even possible to light a fire. You have been protected by Buddhas and devas." Masters Han Shan and Ch'e K'ung thanked them all and said: "One must pass through this [before reaching the goal]." They boiled snow and offered drinks to everyone. The next day people on the mountains heard that the two masters were safe and brought them rice, flour, dried fruit and cakes. There was no room for them to stand [inside the hut]. Later, master Han Shan and Miao Feng stayed in the same hut, and, during another heavy snowfall, they both entered the state of Samādhi. Master Han Shan was familiar with living in the midst of ice and snow at Dragon Gate, but he did not relate his experience in his autobiography.'

My thirty-second year (1577–8)

In the spring I left Yen Men [to return to Five Peak Mountain]. I thought of the great debt of gratitude I owed to my parents, a debt I could not pay and which hindered my progress in the Dharma. When I saw the text of master Nan Yao Szu's great vow,[1] I decided to cut my arm to get blood which I would mix with gold powder to write a copy of *The Avataṁsaka Sūtra*. My purpose was to establish a happy connection with the Prajñā from above and to redeem my immense debt [to my parents] here below.[2]

Before I made the above decision, the empress mother invited Buddhist monks to recite sūtras for the protection of the country. I put my name on the list of those [who accepted] and, when she learned of my decision to copy the sūtra [with my own blood], she kindly gave me gold paper for the purpose. The next year in the fourth month, I began writing. At the time master Ch'e K'ung was returning to Kuang Shan Mountain and I presented him with ten poems.

My thirty-third year (1578–9)

I had a mind only for writing the sūtra; each dot and stroke, whether heavy or fine, when written on the paper was followed by my calling the Buddha's name. Monks and laymen who visited the mountain were invited to talk. I conversed with them and wrote simultaneously. To those who inquired about me, I spoke a few words. Eminent and old acquaintances were invited to sit on the meditation bed, and conversation was carried on in the usual manner without interfering with my writing. When checked with the text, not a single mistake was found. Each day as usual I did not perceive anything in motion or motionless. Elderly monks, who were my neighbours, wondered at all this. One day they came and deliberately tried to disturb me; they only believed that I made no errors after reading for themselves what I had written. They asked

[1] To deliver the spirits of his dead parents in order to repay his debt of gratitude.
[2] Readers are advised to avoid a materialistic interpretation of *above* and *below*.

D

Miao Feng: 'How can master Cheng Yin do this?' Miao Feng replied: 'My friend is familiar with the state of Samādhi.'

During my stay on the mountain and until the time of copying the sūtra, I frequently had good dreams:

First, one night I dreamed of entering a Diamond Cave which had a stone door bearing an inscription showing that it was the Great Prajñā temple. Upon entering I saw that it was as extensive as space. The temple buildings and upper chambers were of incomparable majesty. In the central temple there was only a great meditation bed against which I saw the great master Ch'ing Liang lying down and leaning, while Miao Feng stood on his left. I entered quickly and prostrated myself [at the feet of Ch'ing Liang] before going to stand on his right. His instruction was:

'One begins by entering the state of the intermerging Dharmadhātu, which is the interpermeating of Buddha-lands with interwoven hosts and companions and motionless coming and going.'

As he talked, the very state of which he spoke appeared before my eyes, and I felt as if my body and mind joined and merged with it. After the revelation Miao Feng asked the great master: 'Sir, what is this state?' The great master smiled and said: 'This is the state of no state.'

When I awoke, I noticed that my mind and the surrounding objects seemed to be melting and merging into each other without any hindrance.

Another night in a dream, I saw my body rise in the sky until it reached highest space. When it descended there was nothing anywhere but flat land like a crystal mirror shining throughout. Seen from a distance there was only a spacious upper chamber as immense as space itself. Inside the chamber appeared all men, animals, market places and worldly doings without any hindrance in their coming and going. In the centre was a high seat of blazing red gold. I thought it was a Diamond Throne. The beauty and majesty of the chamber were beyond compare. With joy I wished to get near it, and I thought that in such an invigorating state there was filthy disorder. As this thought came into my mind, the chamber became more distant. Then, I thought to myself: 'The clean and unclean are only created by my mind,' and the chamber came nearer. In a moment I saw that monks were standing in line before the seat; they were very tall and incomparably grave and dignified. Suddenly a bhikṣu, holding a sūtra in his hand, came from behind the seat and descended the steps. Giving the sūtra to me, he said: 'The abbot will talk about this sūtra and orders me to give it to you.' I received the sūtra and opened it. It was in Sanskrit which I did not understand and was written in gold. I put it in the pocket [of my sleeve] and asked: 'Who is the abbot?' He replied: 'Maitreya.'[1] I was delighted, followed the bhikṣu, and ascended the stairs. When I reached the steps of the chamber, I closed my eyes, concentrated on my mind, and stood waiting there. Suddenly I heard the sound of a ch'ing, opened my eyes and saw Maitreya already on the throne. I saluted him reverently, looked up, and saw his bright red gold face which was without compare. After saluting him, I thought that since the talk was to be made especially for me, my nature was qualified for it. Therefore, I prostrated myself before him and took out the sūtra which I opened. I heard him say:

'Discrimination is consciousness and non-discrimination is wisdom. Clinging to consciousness causes defilement and accord with wisdom ensures purity. Defilement causes birth and death whereas purity leads to where there are no Buddhas.'

At that moment my body and mind suddenly became void, but I heard his voice ringing distinctly in the air. When I awoke the speech still rang in my ears. Henceforth, I thoroughly understood the difference between consciousness and wisdom. I realised that the place where I had been was Maitreya Buddha's Chamber in the Tuṣita Heaven.

Another night in a dream, I saw a monk who came to report to me: 'Bodhisattva Mañjuśrī has prepared a bath for you on the North Peak. Please come with me.' I followed this messenger and when I arrived I saw a large, quiet hall where the air was filled with

[1] Maitreya is the Buddhist Messiah or the next Buddha now in the Tuṣita Heaven who is to come 5,000 years after the Nirvāṇa of Śākyamuni.

fragrance. All the attendants were monks. I was led to a bathing room where I removed my garments and was ready to bathe. Someone was already in the bath and, as it turned out, the person was a girl. I abhorred the sight and had no desire to bathe. The girl in the bath deliberately changed her appearance and became a man. I joined him and we both bathed. Taking some water he poured it over my head and it entered my body as if washing out a barrel of flesh. It washed out the five viscera leaving only a skinny trunk similar to a crystal cage which was transparent and could be seen through. Then, the man in the bath called for tea, and I saw a monk appear holding half a skull, like half a melon. I looked at it and saw the dripping brain and marrow. The sight of all this was repulsive, but the monk picked up some of the brain with his fingers to show me and said: 'Is this not clean?' Then he put it into my mouth and I swallowed it. As he picked up and put the contents of the skull into my mouth, I swallowed. It tasted like honey. In this way the brain was completely eaten, and now only the blood remained. The man in the bath said: 'You can give it to him' and the monk handed it to me. I received and drank it; it tasted like amṛta [ambrosia]. As the liquid went down my throat it streamed out through all my pores. After the drink, the monk rubbed my back and thumped me, so that I awoke drenched in perspiration. The five viscera were cleansed [from impurities]. Henceforth, my body and mind were as if bathed and were blissful beyond all description.

My dreams were about saints and sages and most of them were auspicious. Thus the Buddha's saying: 'Good dreams are frequent' was trustworthy.

My thirty-fourth year (1579–80)
In the autumn the building of Ta Tzu Shou temple in the capital was completed. At first the empress mother had wanted to repair T'a Yuan temple and its Śarīra stūpa at Five Peak Mountain to accumulate merits for the happiness of [her husband] the late emperor's spirit and for the protection of [her son] the present emperor. The government had been ordered to carry out her wishes, but because Five Peak Mountain was so far from the capital, it was decided

(without consulting the empress mother) to choose a nearer site where Ta Tzu Shou temple was erected. When the building was completed, a report was presented to her, but the empress mother found that her wishes regarding [T'a Yuan temple at] Five Peak Mountain had not been fulfilled and ordered her son to send a court official to take three thousand men to the mountain to repair the temple and stūpa there.

It was thus the first time that the court undertook to do Buddha-work and that a court official was sent outside [the palace]. I was apprehensive that if he could not complete the work properly, some harm to the Dharma-door might result. Therefore, I undertook to give a helping hand and everything was done satisfactorily.

My thirty-fifth year (1580–1)

That year, by imperial order, all lands were to be surveyed for the imposition of a land tax throughout the country. Five Peak Mountain had always been exempt from all taxes, but clever villains concealed the truth, hoping to levy a tax of five hundred piculs of rice on the region. Orders were repeatedly received for a declaration of the taxable land. Those living in the monasteries and in the huts were alarmed, and thus all Five Peak Mountain seemed on the point of becoming a fox's lair. Senior monks told me about this; I said: 'Venerable Sirs, please keep quiet and don't worry. Let's think it over and see how to deal with it.' Then I arranged to send a petition to the authorities, and the proposed survey was cancelled. Thus all the sacred places at Five Peak Mountain were spared.

My thirty-sixth year (1581–2)

A Mokṣa Pariṣad[1] was held. Earlier Miao Feng also (like me) had cut his arm for blood to write a copy of *The Avataṁsaka Sūtra*; now both of us had taken the same vow to organise a complete ceremonial meeting, called Mokṣa Pariṣad. Miao Feng collected subscriptions and, when funds and provisions were ready, five hundred

[1] A great assembly for the confession of sins, the inculcation of morality and discipline, and the distribution of charity.

well-known and virtuous monks were invited from the capital. All arrangements were completed for the meeting.

It happened that at the same time, the emperor ordered [Taoist] prayers for the birth of an heir to the throne and sent an official to Wu Tang; whereas the empress mother sent another official to Five Peak Mountain. At the monastery I thought that, among the Buddha-works performed by the monks which were for the prosperity of the country and protection of the imperial rule, prayers for the birth of an heir to the throne were for the foundation of the state and nothing was more important by comparison. Instead of the Mokṣa Pariṣad which would be performed in our own names, I was willing to reserve the preparations, which had already been made, for prayers for the birth of an heir to the throne. Miao Feng did not understand my idea nor apparently did the official [sent by the empress mother], his motive being only to win the emperor's favour by flattery. I stuck to and fought for my idea but the official was displeased and criticised me. It then became known that I had disobeyed the court envoy. A short while later a wizard of Chiang Nan created difficulties and those who were against the prayer meeting intended to use him as a pretext to create trouble for us in order to prevent our holding it. However, because of the genuineness of the prayer meeting, the sole purpose of which was for the birth of the heir to the throne, no harm could be done to it.

That year because the stūpa was now completely repaired, I placed in it my copy of *The Avataṁsaka Sūtra* with a copy of the text of my own vows.

I also collected subscriptions for the installation of revolving sūtra shelves and for all that was required during the meeting, such as articles used for worship, implements, provisions, and the like. Miao Feng was in the capital and knew nothing of all this. I made these preparations myself and spent ninety days and nights without a wink of sleep.

In the tenth month when the date of the meeting drew near, Miao Feng arrived with over five hundred invited monks. Thus there were assembled in the monastery one thousand people, including guests. I had to provide all of them with food, drink and lodging; all this was done without confusion. Not knowing from where these facilities came, those present were amazed.

At the beginning, there was the Festival of Water and Land which lasted seven days and nights, during which I did not eat a grain of rice and drank only water. Nevertheless, I attended to all the work completely. Offerings to Buddhas and Bodhisattvas were changed every day, and there were five hundred tables; all was done carefully without any mistake. Visitors thought that all this was transported by the gods, but I knew that we had the Buddha's aid.

Commentary by disciple Fu Cheng

The emperor sent a court official to the Taoist priests at Wu Tang requesting prayers that Lady Cheng give birth to an heir to the throne. The empress mother sent another official to Five Peak Mountain requesting Buddhist prayers for Lady Wang Ts'ai Jen[1] to give birth to an heir to the throne. Thus mother and son had both different religious beliefs and different wishes. In order not to get into trouble, the court official, who was sent to Five Peak Mountain and knew the emperor's wishes, dared not incur his displeasure. Therefore, he was disloyal to the empress mother and refused to approve of the prayers for the birth of an heir to be performed at what was to have been a Mokṣa Pariṣad. As for Miao Feng, he could not understand why prayers for the heir should be performed at a meeting which had an essentially different purpose. Master Han Shan stuck to his belief that the foundation of the state should have priority. He personally made the

[1] Both Lady Cheng and Lady Wang Ts'ai Jen were wives of the emperor who loved the former but not the latter. Therefore, he ordered Taoist priests to pray for Lady Cheng to give birth to the heir. The empress mother seemed to have preferred Lady Wang Ts'ai Jen, who might have been more virtuous, and asked Buddhist monks to pray that she give birth to the heir. According to the Chinese custom at the time, the baby born first would become the heir to the throne, and, naturally the mother of the heir would have an important position in the palace; she would be the mother of the next emperor of the country.

arrangements and spent ninety days and nights without a wink of sleep. The invited monks met, and for seven days the master drank only water without eating a grain of rice. The performance of all the works, including the offerings that were made, could only have been achieved with aid given by the Buddhas and through the brightness [i.e. the effectiveness] of the master's Samādhi. Later when trouble came at Lao Shan, the emperor said: 'The whole court was for the monks and I alone for the Taoists.' The above lines conclude the story of the prayers that were given simultaneously at Wu Tang and Five Peak Mountain.

My thirty-seventh year (1582–3)

That spring I lectured on *The Hua Yen Hsuen T'an* [a commentary on *The Avataṁsaka Sūtra* by state master Ch'ing Liang]. For one hundred days a large gathering of monks and laymen came from everywhere. Each day ten thousand people were provided with meals. At mealtime there was perfect order, and just as during the lecture, no noise was heard; all was accomplished under my personal and unassisted supervision. No one knew how all this came about, but my energy was spent on the meeting.

After the assembly, all that was left, including money and provisions worth approximately ten thousand coins, was handed over to the monastery for its running expenses. Equipped with our rice bowls, Miao Feng and I left for a long journey. He went to Lu Ya, but because I was indisposed, I proceeded to Chang Shih Yen in the Chen Ting district for a rest. I wrote a poem containing the following lines:

'A cliff leaning against the sky would halt the sun.
Leap then when the road is cut by a precipice.'[1]

That year in the eighth month, the heir to the throne was born.[2] I went to Chung Feng monastery west of the capital where I supervised the carving of wooden blocks for printing the *Preface* for *The*

[1] The master knew that he had incurred the emperor's displeasure and decided to leave Five Peak Mountain in order to avoid trouble.
[2] The heir was born to Lady Wang Ts'ai Jen.

Sayings of Chung Feng. That winter I performed ceremonies of offerings to water at Shih Shih.

My thirty-eighth year (1583-4)

In the first month the ceremonies of offerings to water were completed. Because of the well-known Five Peak Mountain prayer meeting for the birth of an heir to the throne, I realised that it would be inconvenient for me to live in the midst of such fame. I went to Tung Hai [Eastern Sea] where I adopted my alias Han Shan and dropped the use of my name Cheng Yin.

Immediately after the destruction of my monastery by fire (when I was 21), I had made a resolution to rebuild it and had continued my practice [of Dharma] while waiting for an opportune moment. During my eight years on Five Peak Mountain, I had had several chances to carry out my plan. I was now afraid that if I were to go too far away I would lose any further opportunities; hence my decision to live at Tung Hai. This was my original intention.

On the eighth day of the fourth month, I arrived at Lao Shan Mountain. When I parted with Miao Feng, he did not think that I could continue alone and told his disciple Teh Tsung to accompany and serve me. I accepted his kind offer.

Now I had read in another *Commentary* by master Ch'ing Liang on *The Avataṁsaka Sūtra* a chapter on the Bodhisattvas' abode which said: 'At Tung Hai there is a place called the Nārāyaṇa Cave where since the earliest time Bodhisattvas came to dwell.' Master Ch'ing Liang's *Commentary* read: 'The Sanskrit word *Nārāyana* means *firm* and *stable*. It is Lao Shan [stable or firm mountain] at Tung Hai. According to the guide book *Yu Kung*, there still exists a cave somewhere between Teng Chou and Lai Chou in the Ching Chou district.'

Since I had the place in my mind, I went to see it. I found Lao Shan Mountain without difficulty but it was uninhabitable. Therefore, I went along the south side to where there was a deep valley with all the mountains behind it and the great sea in front. The place was strange and unique, appearing not to belong to our world. It was called The Avalokiteśvara Shrine and really was an ancient temple in ruins with only its foundation remaining. I examined it and discovered that in the beginning of the Yuan dynasty [1280–1341] seven Taoists had been there and falsely used emperor Shih Tsu's name to usurp Buddhist properties which they then converted into Taoist temples. Upon the emperor's return from a punitive expedition to the West, Buddhist monks petitioned him and regained their property. No one cared for Lao Shan Mountain because it was isolated by the seashore; thus the temple stood abandoned and in ruins. I liked the place's loneliness which made it ideal for a recluse and wanted to stay there. At first I used only a mat as shelter under a tree; seven months later upāsaka Chang Ta Hsin, a native of the district, built a thatched hut for me. I stayed there with great enjoyment for a year but made no acquaintance. At the time, Dharma-master Kuei Feng of Ling Shan monastery at Chi Mo, who was the Dharma Eye of the region, was my only friend.

Commentary by disciple Fu Cheng

The name of Five Peak Mountain became famous because the prayer meeting for the birth of the heir to the throne had been a grand affair. Furthermore, by incurring the displeasure of the court official, its name became even more famous. This is why the place became uninhabitable [for master Han Shan] and explains the inadvisability of [his] moving even to a nearby monastery. The only solution was to go to the remote Lao Shan Mountain at Tung Hai.

At first the master had gone from Pao En monastery to the [northern] capital to fulfil his vow to rebuild his monastery. Later, his journey from Five Peak Mountain to the capital was made for the same reason, as was his more recent journey from the capital until he obtained the donation of *The Tripiṭaka* for the monastery[1] and petitioned for a reduction of the court's expenses[2] in order to provide a fund for the rebuilding of the monastery; all this he did for the same reason. This is why he wrote: 'This was my original intention.'

[1][2] See 1589–90.

My thirty-ninth year (1584-5)

That autumn in the ninth month, the empress mother sent for the sponsors of the prayer meeting that had been held for the birth of an heir to the throne, master Ta Fang, Miao Feng and me. Master Ta Fang and Miao Feng were duly rewarded, but the empress mother failed to locate me. She had sent Tuan An, abbot of Lung Hua monastery, to look for me. Knowing that I was at the seashore, he came to see me. He informed me of her majesty's desire to reward me, but I said: 'If her majesty allows me to spend my old age here, I shall be amply rewarded. I need nothing else.' The abbot transmitted my reply to her majesty who then decided to appropriate some land on the Western Hill for building a temple for me. A court official was sent to insist that I accept the offer, but I declined. The official returned and reported to her majesty that my decision to stay where I was was irrevocable. She forgave me and, hearing that I did not have a suitable dwelling place, gave three thousand gold coins for rebuilding the temple [at Lao Shan Mountain by the sea]. When the official arrived, I stopped him, saying: 'I already have enough huts to make me happy. There is no point in making new additions.' I declined the offer, but the official insisted, saying that he dared not deliver my reply to her majesty. I told him: 'The ancients could amend edicts for the relief of famine victims. There is a famine now in Shantung province. Why not extend her majesty's mercy to these starving people?' I then ordered monks to accompany the court envoy to various places where donations were distributed to monks, helpless old people, and prisoners. The books used for entering the donations were delivered to her majesty who was greatly pleased and deeply moved. Later, when I got into difficulty and was brought before the district court,[1] the magistrate questioned me concerning my 'misappropriation' of court funds; I asked him to refer to the accounts in the court treasury. When it was discovered that there was only an item relating to the famine relief and nothing else, the emperor clearly saw the falseness of the accusation.

[1] See 1595-6.

Commentary by disciple Fu Cheng

The so-called court funds were not paid directly by the court treasury. They really consisted of money saved from daily expenses allotted for food for the empress mother and the ladies of the court.[1] These expenses were reduced to provide a fund for rebuilding Pao En monastery. This was a good cause and had nothing to do with the inquiry ordered.[2] All this was caused by court intrigue.

My fortieth year (1585–6)

The inhabitants of this eastern district of Tung Hai knew nothing about the Saṅgha. I lived in the mountain where the Huang clan was the largest. Its members came gradually into contact with me. What was now known as the heretical Lo Ching [cult][3] was native to Ch'eng Yang at the foot of the mountain which had been its birthplace before it spread eastward to where the Triratna[4] was completely unknown. I was on the mountain and undertook to convert these people. In time their master led his followers to see me and they began to know the Buddha-Dharma.

My forty-first year (1586–7)

That year collections of *The Tripiṭaka* were distributed to various monasteries. At first *The Tripiṭaka* did not contain certain works that had been written in China. The empress mother ordered that they be added and wooden printing blocks were carved. When the printing was completed, the emperor ordered that fifteen sets be given to well-known monasteries throughout the country. Four were sent to four monasteries of the bordering regions: Lao Shan at Tung Hai [Eastern Sea], P'u T'o on Nan Hai [Southern Sea], O Mei in western Szechwen and Lu Ya in the North.

[1] See 1589–90.
[2] See 1595–6.
[3] A corrupted form of Taoism.
[4] The Three Treasures: Buddha, Dharma and Saṅgha.

At the time the empress mother still remembered the [famous] Five Peak Mountain prayer meeting, and, as I had repeatedly refused to come and accept her reward, she sent a set of The Tripiṭaka to Tung Hai for me. I did not know anything about this donation, and, when it arrived, there was no room for it. Therefore, it was kept temporarily at the office of the district magistrate. When I saw the imperial order accompanying The Tripiṭaka, I went to the capital to express my gratitude. The empress mother also ordered all the court ladies to give donations for repairing the temple for the reception of The Tripiṭaka. She ordered that the temple at Tung Hai be renamed Hai Yin [Ocean Symbol].

In the capital I heard that master Ta Kuan had gone to see me at Lao Shan and I hurriedly returned there. When I reached the foot of the mountain, I met him as he was coming down. Together we returned to my place where we stayed for twenty days. He presented me with a poem which contained these lines:

'Leisurely I came by the seashore to dwell and dropped
East of the mountain the heavy burden of my fame.'[1]

That winter in the eleventh month after a long period of incessant and fatiguing work which had continued since I was thirty-six years old, I finally found real rest in the new meditation hall that enabled me to lay down all conceptions of body and mind and find an incomparable bliss. One evening I sat in meditation and, when I got up during the night, I saw that the sea was limpid and the space [above it] was completely clear [and] in a great brightness within which there was not a single thing. Thereupon, I recited the following gāthā:

'In clear space and the limpid sea the moon shines on the snow
Wiping out all traces of the saintly and the worldly.'[2]

[1] After making a good reputation at Five Peak Mountain, Han Shan went to the seashore to forget all about it; he was free from attachment to all worldly things.
[2] The moon stands for enlightenment, the state in which all dualities have no room.

When the Eye of Diamond opens all the flowers in the sky
Vanish while the great earth returns to stillness and extinction.'[1]

I returned to the hall and seeing *The Śūraṅgama Sūtra* on the desk,
I opened it at random and read the following sentence:

'Your body and mind as well as external mountains, rivers, space
and the great earth are but phenomena within the wondrous
bright True Mind.'

Thus the whole sūtra's field of insight became clear to me, and I
ordered a brush and paper to write my book *The Hanging Mirror of
The Śūraṅgama Sūtra*. It was finished when only half a candle had
burned. The evening meditation in the hall was just ending. I called
for the Karmadāna[2] to come and read the manuscript to me. It was
as if the words were being spoken in a dream.

Commentary by disciple Fu Cheng

In another book, master Han Shan wrote:
'All know that there is nothing but illusion. One should know
how to make use of illusion in order not to be turned round by it.
One day during my stay at Hai Yin temple [at Tung Hai], I
remembered the story of a man who came one night to chop off
the head of Patriarch Lu.[3] I decided to practise the Patriarch's
samādhibala.[4] Every night I left the door open while I sat in
meditation, ready to give my head to anyone who might wish to
"borrow" it. Gradually I felt that I had made progress in that
direction. Suddenly one night I was informed of a robber's visit
and said: "Show him in." I sat erect in the candlelight and was
not the least perturbed. When he reached the door, the robber
hesitated and dared not enter. Nevertheless, he was a tall fellow.

[1] 'Eye of Diamond' stands for prajñā or wisdom; 'flowers' for the phenomenal
which is illusory; and 'stillness and extinction' for Nirvāṇa which is not
attained until prajñā pierces the unreality of all things.
[2] Duty distributor, second in command in a monastery.
[3] The Sixth Patriarch's lay surname.
[4] The power of Samādhi to overcome all disturbing thoughts, including fear.

I called to him and said: "There is nothing here." Then I ordered that two hundred small coins be taken from the cellar and given to him. If I had not been prepared for the incident, I might have been frightened.

'Another evening I entered the state of Samādhi wherein space and time were void; the Ocean Symbol[1] emitted light; and mountains and rivers shook. I acquired the [corresponding] wisdom [that accompanies Samādhi]; a short while later, I awakened and entered the most important state [that is described] in *The Śūraṅgama Sūtra*, beholding it clearly. Then I hurried to light a candle and write of my experience. My hand did not stop during the entire fifth watch that night[2] at the end of which time *The Hanging Mirror of The Śūraṅgama Sūtra* was finished. The attendant came and was surprised to see the lighted candle on the desk at such an early hour.'

My forty-second year (1587–8)

That year repairs were made to the temple and when they were completed, the hall was opened for me to teach the Buddhist precepts to followers of the faith. After the opening of the hall, monks came from all directions. I gave to the Buddhist laymen who attended *A Straight Talk on the Heart Sūtra*.[3]

That autumn in the eighth month, district magistrate Hu [An Shun], who had resigned his post and returned to his native place, brought his relative's son to me in order that the young man could leave home to become a monk, and serve me as my attendant. I gave him the name of Fu Shan.

Commentary by disciple Fu Cheng

When the master went to the eastern district, I had an opportunity to meet his attendant and secretary Fu Shan, also called Chih Wei. In the Tsung Ching hall of Chin Tzu temple, I saw him every

---

[1] See 1564–5.
[2] From 3 to 5 a.m.
[3] Cf *Ch'an and Zen Teaching, First Series*, pp. 207–23. Rider, London.

morning and evening; we were both in the same 'profound way'. He assisted the master as secretary and compiled *Master Han Shan's Journey to the East*. He was the master's best and unsurpassed pupil, following him in times of difficulty and danger. All notes and records in the book came from his own hand. His relative, ex-magistrate Hu An Shun, was a native of the Tung Hai district. As a result of a former cause, Bhikṣu Fu Shan was sent to Hai Yin temple at Lao Shan to become a monk. Later he stayed at Wu Ju monastery and became abbot of Fa Yun monastery at Kuang Shan. At the age of seventy, he passed away while seated in meditation.

My forty-third year (1588–9)

One day as a disciple read my *The Hanging Mirror of The Śūraṅgama Sūtra*, he said to me: 'This sūtra deals clearly with the [inward] seeing of the mind, but does not eliminate words and letters entirely. I am afraid future students will have difficulty penetrating its profound meaning. I hope that each word will merge into the seeing mind, thereby bringing about the almsgiving of the Buddha-Dharma.' I then decided to write *The Thorough Meaning of The Śūraṅgama Sūtra* [Len Yen Ching Tung I].[1] Although I had conceived the outline, I did not yet write the manuscript.

My forty-fourth year (1589–90)

That year I read *The Tripiṭaka* and gave lectures on *The Lotus Sūtra* and *The Awakening of Faith*. Ever since leaving Five Peak Mountain, I had thought of visiting my parents. I was afraid that I might fall into worldly ways but for the time being I wanted to have a try at testing myself. One evening while I was sitting in meditation, the following lines came to me by chance:

'Each day as smoke curls up into the cold of
      Space, birds and fishes wander in one mirror.[2]

[1] My translation of *The Śūraṅgama Sūtra* (Rider, London) is based on Han Shan's work.
[2] When the mind is frozen by meditation, it is like a great mirror in which all phenomena appear and vanish.

Last night the moon sank suddenly beyond the sky[1]
To mingle its lone brightness with the black dragon's.'[2]

I called my attendant and said to him: 'I am returning to my native village to see my old parents.'

That winter in the tenth month, since I had solicited *The Tripiṭaka* for Pao En monastery, I went first to the capital and requested it. The emperor ordered the donation. I received it and began my return journey. In the eleventh month I arrived at Lung Chiang where day after day the stūpa emitted light. On the day of *The Tripiṭaka*'s arrival, the stūpa sent northward a long ray that resembled a bridge. The monks who were sent out to receive the sūtras walked in the light and followed its direction. When the sūtras were placed in the shelves, a ceremonial meeting was held; the light continued for days without interruption. Those who witnessed this event numbered over ten thousand daily. Everyone took it for a rare and auspicious sign.

As soon as my mother heard that I was returning, she sent a messenger to inquire about the date of my arrival. I said: 'I am coming for the Court and not for my family. When my mother sees me, if she is joyful as she was at the time of our parting, I will remain at home for two nights; otherwise I will not return.' When my mother heard this, she said: 'A meeting that is like a second birth for us is to take place! It will fill me with great joy. Why should I be sad? One meeting would be enough, and now he says he will stay for two nights!'

Upon my return, when my mother saw me she was extremely happy and in little fits of laughter. I was greatly surprised when during the evening's conversation in which an elderly clansman

[1] The 'moon beyond the sky' stands for Enlightenment, outside the realm of birth and death, or beyond the sky which is phenomenal.
[2] The black dragon had a highly prized pearl under its jaw. The first two lines deal with samsaric activities as reflected in the Great-Mirror-Wisdom. The last two lines forecast the temporary absence of the bright moon—or Enlightenment—which sank into the ocean of saṁsāra to meet the black dragon that had the bright pearl, Han Shan's mother who also was free from worldly attachment.

asked whether I came by boat or road, mother said: 'Why ask about whether his return was by road or boat?' The elder asked: 'Where does he come from?' Mother replied: 'He came from space.' I was startled and said: 'No wonder my mother could part with me when she did.' I asked her: 'Did you think of me after our parting?' She replied: 'How could I prevent myself?' I asked her: 'How did you rid yourself of the thought?' She said: 'At first I did not know where you were. When I learned that you were at Five Peak Mountain, I asked the monks where it was. They replied: "Under the Great Bear is where your son is staying." Every night after that I worshipped the Great Bear and repeated the Bodhisattva's name. After that [while repeating the Bodhisattva's name], I did not think of you. If I were to hear of your death, I would immediately stop worshipping [the Great Bear] and thinking of you. What I see now must be your transformation body [Nirmāṇakāya].'

The following day I paid reverence to the ancestral tombs, looked for a grave for my parents[1] and found a suitable site. My father was eighty years old, and I said jokingly: 'Today I will bury Father alive in order to avoid returning again later.' I took a mattock and dug in the earth. My old mother snatched it from me and said: 'Let the old lady bury herself. Why trouble others?' She dug in the earth a number of times.[2]

On the third day I said farewell to my parents. My old mother was joyful as usual and did not even frown. I began to see that she was no ordinary person.

At Chi Mo I had a disciple whose name was Huang Na Shan, alias Tzu Kuang. He was subprefect Huang's brother. When I arrived at the seashore, he was nineteen years old and became my disciple. He asked for my instruction and I taught him *The Śūraṅgama Sūtra* which in two months he knew by heart. He then became

[1] It is a Chinese custom to find a suitable grave for one's parents long before their death.
[2] The master's joke was to deliver the old man at once and avoid waiting for his death. The old mother seems to tell her son that she wanted to ferry herself to the 'other shore' because her deliverance could only be effected through her own efforts.

a vegetarian and did not change his mind even in the face of his parents' opposition. He was earnest in his Ch'an practice and his ribs never touched the mat.[1]

While I was returning to the South, Tzu Kuang reflected and said: 'We were born on the borders of the country and for a whole aeon we have not had a chance to hear about the Three Treasures [of Buddha, Dharma and Sangha]. We are fortunate to have met so soon a great master who has come as a friend [even though] un-invited. If he does not return, we will have lost a helper on whom we can rely.' After saying this, he cut the skin of his arm[2] for the lighting of a lamp [to be] offered to worship Avalokiteśvara Bodhisattva, who was called upon to protect me for an early return. Although the burn was painful, he sat in a dignified attitude, repeating the Bodhisattva's name day and night. Three months later the burn had healed, leaving a scar that resembled the [complete form of the] Bodhisattva, including eyes, eyebrows, body and clothes, as clearly recognisable as [they would be] if drawn for a picture. Not even his mother and wife knew anything about all this. He asked to leave his home to become a monk but I refused. Then he said: 'I have turned a somersault.[3] Why do you stop me?' This showed that even in this worthless and miserable region the seed of Buddhahood had not ceased to grow.

Immediately after I had resolved to rebuild the original monastery [that had been destroyed by fire], I had gone to stay at Five Peak Mountain; and although there had been some chances of my plan materialising, it would have involved an expenditure of a few hundred thousand [gold] coins, which would not have been easy to raise. This is why I waited by the sea for an opportune time. When the plan was ripe for execution, I took advantage of the transporting of *The Tripiṭaka* to the southern capital [Nanking] to write a detailed petition for rebuilding the monastery which I presented to

[1] He ceased to sleep at night.
[2] It is very likely that Tzu Kuang used a small piece of cloth soaked with vegetable oil and rolled up like a candle, which he planted on his arm where the skin was cut. This was an expression of his earnestness in his prayers.
[3] A Chinese way of saying: 'I have overcome many obstacles.'

the empress mother. I mentioned the large amount of money that
would be needed for this difficult and great work and entreated her
to reduce by one hundred taels her daily expenses for food, thus
ensuring that the project could be started within three and be
finished within ten years. She was very pleased and ordered the
saving of the money to begin on the twelfth month of that year.

My forty-fifth year (1590–1)

In the spring of that year, I copied out *The Lotus Sūtra* to pay my
debt of gratitude to the empress mother.

At the time a plot was hatched by those who wished to usurp the
Buddhist temples. They joined with Taoist priests and falsely
claimed that their Taoist temples had been seized. They gathered
together many people and demanded justice at the headquarters of
the viceroy of the province. Viceroy Li, who knew of the plot and
hated the plotters, sent the case to Lai Chou prefecture for exhaust-
ive investigation. I was present and worked against the plotters.

The rascals numbered a few hundred and caused a furious
clamour in the town. At one time I found myself surrounded by
them; I had two attendants with me but dismissed them and walked
on slowly alone. The chief of the devils flourished a chopper and
danced in front of me as if he wanted to kill me. I smiled, looked at
him and said: 'You want to kill people, but how will you justify it?'
He became uneasy and sheathed his blade. When I had walked round
the walled town with him for over two [Chinese] miles I was on the
point of parting company with him. However, the maddened
crowd became suspicious and, thinking that he was betraying them,
was about to assault him. I thought: 'If these rioters attack him, he
will be in immediate danger. What can I do?' Hesitating as I was
about to leave him, I dragged him to my place, closed the door and
told him to change his clothes. We assumed a self-possessed attitude,
talking and laughing, and took out a melon and other fruits which
we ate. Now the whole town was alive with the rumour that the
Taoist priests had killed Buddhist monks. When the prefect heard
of this, he sent constables to arrest the rioters. They became frightened, kow-towed, and begged me to save them. I said to them:

'Don't be frightened; wait for the result of my talk.' When the prefect arrived, he asked: 'Didn't the rioters murder Buddhist monks?' I replied: 'They did not.' Although he had come to arrest the rioters, he saw Buddhist monks and the leader of the rascals sitting together eating melons and other fruits. The prefect asked: 'Why all this clamour?' I replied: 'The noise comes from the marketplace.' Since he intended to put the rioters in jail, I told him: 'My idea is to disperse them. Jailing would keep them all together in the same place.' He understood and ordered the local authorities to drive the rioters away. In less than three days, all of them had scattered and order prevailed again.

That year I wrote my commentary *A Study of Lao-Tze and Chuang Tze* [Kuan Lao Chuang Ying Hsiang Lun].

My forty-sixth year (1591-2)
That year by order of the empress mother, a statue of Vairocana was made in sandalwood and the building of the great hall was completed. In the autumn my disciple Huang Tzu Kuang died while sitting in meditation.

My forty-seventh year (1592-3)
That autumn in the seventh month, I went to the capital and visited master Ta Kuan at his abode on the mountain. It was there that in the Chin dynasty Dharma-master Ching Wan, who was worried that the Buddha-Dharma would disappear after the three calamities which he anticipated in the coming kalpa of destruction, undertook to carve stone sūtras which were stored in a grotto. The stūpa and temple had been sold by the monks there and were now redeemed by master Ta Kuan.

Master Ta Kuan thought of me because he wanted me to record the story in writing. As I happened to arrive at the same moment, he was extremely delighted. Together we went to the mountain of the Stone Sūtras, and I wrote the story of Dharma-master Ching Wan's stūpa and temple and of the replacing of relics in the grotto; I also put in order the manuscripts that I had written at Hai Yin temple.

I had the most wonderful time of my life with master Ta Kuan; both of us sat face to face for forty days and nights [in a state of deep Samādhi].

Commentary by disciple Fu Cheng

In the Fang Shan district there was a grotto where stone sūtras were stored. In the Sui dynasty [A.D. 590–617] Dharma-master Ching Wan used stone blocks for carving sūtras of *The Tripiṭaka* and stored them in the grotto behind a stone door. During the successive generations more stone tablets were carved. After master Ta Kuan took charge of the grotto, a monk of Shih Teng temple at Tu Ch'eng, who had raised subscriptions in the South, had more carvings made.

Because I had gone to the capital for an examination in the forty-sixth year of the Wan Li reign, I assisted with the work in the grotto.

I heard of the following story from master Han Shan's attendant at Wu Ju:

'In the twentieth year [1592–3] of the Wan Li reign, masters Han Shan and Ta Kuan met in a garden of the western suburb of the town of Tu Men. For forty days and nights, they sat motionless face to face without sleeping. As they planned to compile *The Transmission of the Lamp* for the Ming dynasty, they set a time for a journey to Ts'ao Ch'i [where the monastery of the Sixth Patriarch was] to dredge the rivulet for the purpose of reopening the Dharma-vein.'

In his autobiography master Han Shan merely wrote 'I had a wonderful time' without giving any details. This probably was not wonderful enough for him since there were more wonders in his lifetime.

My forty-eighth year (1593–4)

That year there was a severe famine in Shantung province where bodies of the starved lay in the streets. All the monastery's provisions were distributed to the starving people near the mountain, but this soon proved inadequate. Consequently, I sailed in a boat to Liao Tung to purchase a few hundred piculs of beans to relieve the suffering. Because of this there soon was not a single person dying of starvation in the four hamlets on our side of the mountain.

My forty-ninth year (1594-5)

That spring in the third month, viceroy Cheng K'un Yai of Shan-tung came to the mountain to visit me and inquire about the Dharma. I expounded it to him in a manner suitable to his understanding.

That winter in the tenth month, I went to the capital to offer my congratulations to the empress mother. I was kept there to pass the new year in the capital where I was asked to lecture on the Buddhist precepts at Tzu Shou temple.

Knowing that the empress mother's savings for the rebuilding of Pao En monastery had reached an appreciable amount, I asked her to have the work begun. The question was left unresolved since the Japanese were then invading Korea and it was decided to send a punitive expedition there.

Commentary by disciple Fu Cheng

The congratulations to the empress mother were presented on the occasion of the winter solstice festival. Her request for lectures on the Buddhist precepts gave the master an opportunity to end his connections with the construction of Tzu Shou temple in the capital which had been decided upon in the seventh year of this reign. As for the rebuilding of Pao En monastery, the empress mother's savings had reached a substantial amount and the plan was on the verge of materialising when it fell into abeyance. This concluded a period of journeys to the North for this noble purpose. His autobiography relates the whole affair from beginning to end. If he had not had the rebuilding of the monastery in mind, he would not have gone to the capital to present his congratulations to the empress mother; and, if he had not paid visits to the capital during these three years, he would not have been involved in the trouble that was yet to arise.

I heard the following story from the master's attendant at Tsung Ching hall:

'The empress mother invited master Han Shan to give lectures on the Buddhist precepts and generously gave him donations. Tzu Shou temple was also called Tusiṭa Mountain temple. Its abbot's room was adorned with embroidered hangings and the offerings to Buddha consisted of rare fruits and excellent food that came from everywhere. Clothing, food, articles of worship and implements needed by the abbot were supplied by the court's ceremonial director and were carried along the road in an unbroken stream. Spectators stood in a line like a human wall. Indeed, offerings sent by the court ladies and officials were so generous that their value could not be estimated. All the children who visited the temple were given gifts. Foodstuffs and money given by the court treasury were not accepted; only fifty-three persons who participated in Ch'an meditation practice went out to beg for their own food and they returned every day empty-handed; but in the temple, boxes and baskets were full of gold coin donations and the granary was overflowing with cloth and grain. Every day a few thousand people ate copious meals that had been prepared in the monastery kitchen.

'That year on the eighth day of the twelfth month, the empress mother ordered official Ch'en Ju to send a Vairocana hat, a brocaded purple robe, a pair of Pao Chi shoes, and woollen underwear as gifts to master Han Shan; the master declined to accept them. Three times these gifts were presented and finally he was compelled to accept them; but he never wore them.'

At the time master Ta Kuan stayed on the Stone Sūtras Mountain. One day he opened the grotto and found under a statue of Buddha a container in which had been placed Buddha relics. The empress mother heard of this and ordered an official to make offerings to the relics and also to present a purple robe to master Ta Kuan. For three days offerings were made to the relics which were then put back in the grotto. Master Ta Kuan declined to accept the gift and requested that it be given to master Han Shan. On the occasion he wrote the following gāthā:

'For thirty years by sea and river have I
Travelled with one thin robe in spring and autumn.
I am shy of clothing my poor bones in this purple robe
Which I now pass on to a great man to reap more blessings.'

The day that the robe was given to master Han Shan, the empress ordered the messenger to invite him to the palace so that she could ask him for a Buddhist name for herself. As the master knew that that was not the emperor's idea, he declined the invitation on the ground that monks were forbidden to enter palaces, according to the rules prescribed by their founder. The official was subsequently ordered to bring a picture of the master to the palace along with an inscription of her Buddhist name which would be given to her by him. She ordered that the portrait be hung in the palace and furthermore that the emperor should stand by her side while she prostrated herself before it and received her Buddhist name. Although the emperor was a filial son, he could not suppress his anger on that occasion.

My fiftieth year (1595–6)

That spring in the second month, I left the capital and returned to the sea-shore. Then my misfortunes began. At the start they were due to the court official who was sent out again to deliver *The Tripiṭaka* to me. The emperor did not like him. The performance of Buddhist ceremonies had already caused some inconvenience, and, when the official was sent to Tung Hai, he for some reason incurred the emperor's displeasure which almost spread to the empress mother's entourage. The ministers were apprehensive about all this. It so happened that someone powerful in the court hated the official in charge of delivering *The Tripiṭaka* and wanted to use him as a scapegoat and have him put to death. Taking advantage of the false rumours that had been spread previously by the Taoist priests, a servant of the eastern office of the court security department was ordered to disguise himself as a Taoist priest, beat the court drum,[1] and present a petition to the emperor who read it, was angered, and ordered my arrest. Because the court official was involved in the delivery of *The Tripiṭaka*, he was arrested as well.

I heard of this and met my followers, saying: 'The Buddha did not leave the three miserable worlds [of hells, hungry ghosts and animals] just to save one living being. This Tung Hai region was a small unknown place; the Three Treasures had never been heard of here before. I have spent twelve years teaching and converting the people here, and now even a three-year-old child knows how to repeat the Buddha's name. Whole families and villages have forsaken heresy to return to the right Path. My will is fulfilled and I do not fear death. The only thing that causes me grief is that my plan to rebuild Pao En monastery has not materialised.'

When I left Chi Mo, the people of the town bade me farewell with tears in their eyes, showing that I had won their hearts.

Upon my arrival in the capital, the emperor ordered that I appear before the bureau of pacification. At the interrogation, I was beaten; the head of the bureau, who had received orders in advance to indict me on all counts, questioned me about the empress mother's donations, totalling a few hundred thousand gold coins, to various well-known monasteries. I was tortured but said: 'I regret that as a monk I am unable to requite all favours received from the state. Shall I now regret my life and try to deny the charge thus implying that his majesty is not pious?[2] Even if I were to twist my own ideas to make them fit in with a confession for my own advantage and if I were to obey his majesty's order to injure the constant obligations of morality, this would not be in accord with the love which a subject should have for his sovereign. Furthermore,

[1] Usually a drum was installed outside the palace and was beaten to draw the emperor's attention in case of alarm or injustice.

[2] As a poor monk Han Shan was unable to requite all favours from the state. By denying the charge, he indirectly would be implying the emperor was wrong, did not approve his mother's orders to build monasteries, and thus did not fulfil his filial duty to which in China even an emperor was subject.

what about the historical records of all this?'[1] I fought the case with all my strength, recognising only the donation of over seven hundred gold coins which I requested the emperor to check in the account books of the court. When the accounts were examined, there was no item except the donation for the famine relief. The accusation was proved groundless and the emperor had a clear understanding of the case. From that time, mother and son, empress mother and emperor, were reconciled.

However, after receiving imperial clemency, I was indicted on the charge of illegally building temples, found guilty, and banished to Lei Chou.[2]

That year in the third month when I was put into prison, all the temples and monasteries undertook to recite sūtras and hold Kṣamayati ceremonies[3] for divine aid for me. There were monks who burned their arms with incense sticks and repeated mantras praying for my protection. At Chin Wu the son of subprefect Cheng Fan Ch'i of An Su, whom I did not even know, purposely gave a banquet, to which the nobility and gentry were invited, to gain their support for his efforts to rescue me. With tears in his eyes, he told them of my innocence. All those who were present expressed their regrets for the Dharma. This showed what the popular sentiment towards the Dharma was at the time.

I remained in prison for eight months during which Fa Shan was the only person who provided me with food.

That winter in the tenth month, I was banished to the South. Courtiers and officials, who had dressed themselves to resemble the common people, accompanied me to the river bank. When I left the capital, my attendant Fu Shan and two or three other monks followed me.

In the eleventh month I arrived at Nanking and said farewell to my old mother on the river bank. I wrote a literary composition,

---

[1] Chinese emperors hoped to leave behind a good reputation; they feared the historians who were famous for their sincerity and integrity.

[2] A town in Luichow peninsula, north of Hainan Island and north-east of the Gulf of Tongking.

[3] Seeking forgiveness, patience and indulgence.

Mother and Son. I took with me my nephew K'o Ch'iu who was an orphan.

Earlier when master Ta Kuan and I had passed through the Stone Sūtra grotto, he, thinking of the decline of the Ch'an sect, had said that the source at Ts'ao Ch'i might be obstructed. We had decided to go there to clean it out, but because I was detained by some business, he went ahead and waited for me at Kung Shan. When I was arrested he was staying at Tien Chih; upon hearing the news he was extremely alarmed and said: 'Master Han Shan is finished, but his vow to go to Ts'ao Ch'i is unfinished.' He then went to Ts'ao Ch'i and returned to the capital to report to me on his pilgrimage. When I reached Liao Ch'eng, he learned that I was leaving prison and so returned to Chin Ling [Nanking] to wait for me. After I arrived we had to part company in a temple on the river bank. He wanted to do his utmost to plead my innocence, but I told him: 'The sovereign's order is like that of a father. The subject's obedience is like that of a son. Furthermore, this is a fixed karma. Please do not say anything.' Before we parted he grasped my arm and said: 'When I learned of your trouble during my stay at Tien Chih, I vowed before the Buddha shrine to recite *The Lotus Sūtra* one hundred times for your protection. My mind is your tongue.'[1] I thanked him and departed. He wrote and presented a literary composition to me; it was entitled *The Expulsion of a Guest.*

Commentary by disciple Fu Cheng

When master Han Shan prayed for the birth of an heir to the throne, the news was made known to the court; this was the origin of the trouble which he was able to avoid at the time by going to live by the sea. However, because of his vow to rebuild Pao En monastery he still thought of the capital which he visited

---

[1] Han Shan had asked Ta Kuan not to say anything. Usually if one is arrested wrongly, one should protest with his 'tongue'. Since Han Shan did not protest, Ta Kuan told him that, if his tongue does not protest, Ta Kuan's mind would replace the master's tongue and report it to the Buddha imploring Han Shan's protection.

several times in the next three years. The court's daily saving of money caused a lot of gossip and implicated him. By inviting the empress mother to reduce the court expenses for food by one hundred taels a day for three years, the master inconvenienced the court officials and gave them reason for holding a grudge against him. Since the dynasty's constitution did not allow the empress mother to interfere in the administration of the country, people inside and outside the court took advantage of this to implicate the master.

Because the name of Hai Yin had been given [to the temple at Lao Shan Mountain by the sea] by order of the empress mother and not by the emperor's edict, the master was found guilty of building it illegally. His autobiography did not relate the ordered destruction of that temple, but it was mentioned in his record regarding the stūpa which was erected in memory of master Ta Kuan. Elsewhere the master recorded:

'I was involved in difficulties through spreading the Dharma and incurred His Majesty the Emperor's anger which was as loud as rumbling thunder. I thought that if my old mother heard of this she would be very frightened. Because I was saved from death by His Majesty's clemency and was only banished to Lei Yang, I greeted my mother on the river when I passed through my native village. We were joyful and laughed. Our voices were clear and there was no blocking of the thoughts in our minds and hearts. I asked her: "When you heard of my death, did you worry?" She answered: "Birth and death are fixed by karma. I don't even worry about myself; why should I worry about you? What different people said about you varied so much that my doubts were not set at rest." We waited until dawn, when we were separated again and this for the last time. My mother enjoined: "For the sake of the Dharma, take good care of yourself. Don't worry about me; I am now leaving you for ever." Joyfully she went her way, not even turning her head to see me.'

My fifty-first year (1596–7)

In the first month I crossed Wen Chiang River and paid a visit to imperial counsellor Chou. Upāsaka Wang Hsin Hai of Lu Ling came to pay me his respects on the river and requested me to write a commentary on *The Laṅkāvatāra Sūtra*.

In the second month I climbed Ta Yu Mountain, reached the peak and saw the place where Hui Ming attempted to snatch the Sixth Patriarch's robe. To console him, I composed a poem containing these two lines:

'When thinking now of the ancient stranger's journey through
   The night, what is the mind that passes the peak today?'[1]

Along the road I saw travellers soaked with perspiration and instructed an attendant to erect a booth to offer free tea to passers-by. Because the path was too rugged for pedestrians, I encouraged Buddhist followers there to persuade people to clear it; within a few years it became a level road.

I arrived at Shao Yang and went to the mountain to pay reverence to the Sixth Patriarch. I drank the water of Ts'ao Ch'i and wrote the following gāthā:

'A drop of Ts'ao Ch'i's water coming from the spiritual source
   Flows into the boundless ocean to stir vast waves that lash the sky;
   Few fish change into dragons
   As the source is still most cold.'[2]

The Patriarch's monastery had withered. I could not bear the sight and left with my heart full of sadness.

I arrived at Wu Yang [Canton] and presented myself in prisoner's garb to the military commander who untied my rope, invited me to a vegetarian meal, and found a place for me to stay at Hai Chu temple.

At the time imperial counsellor Chou Ting Shih was giving talks

[1] A comparison between Hui Ming and Han Shan who comes to revive the Ch'an sect.
[2] A drop of the spiritual water at Ts'ao Ch'i flowing into the ocean of Saṁsāra, changing fish (the unenlightened) into dragons (the enlightened). The Ch'an Sect was not prospering in Han Shan's time because Ts'ao Ch'i rivulet was 'cold'.

on Yan Ming metaphysics. When he heard of my arrival, he led a few tens of his followers to call on me. When they were all seated, counsellor Chou began by referring to the saying: 'One can realise the truth only after understanding the condition of day and night.' In the audience a Taoist elder responded: 'The knowing of every man's consciousness functions in his common acts of daily life during the day; the same knowing functions in dreams at night. This is why it is said: "One can realise the truth only after understanding the condition of day and night."' Counsellor Chou said: 'Everyone says that but I am not satisfied with such an interpretation.' He then asked me: 'Venerable old Ch'an Master, please favour us with your view.' I said: 'Where does this sentence come from?' He said: 'It is quoted from *The Book of Changes*' and recited a few sentences. I said: 'This sentence is a Sage's indication to men that they should be awakened to that which is beyond birth and death.' Counsellor Chou applauded and said: 'The old Ch'an Master's interpretation is very clear and in line with the text.' Since his followers did not understand, they asked for further explanation. He said: 'Birth and death are day and night. When one understands the condition of day and night, one will be beyond day and night.' The whole audience applauded.

Before this, the protectors of the Dharma had petitioned viceroy Ch'en of the military prefecture to issue travelling passes for my journey to the South. On the tenth day of the third month, I reached Lei Chou. I wore military uniform[1] and stayed at an ancient temple in the western part of the town.

That summer on the first day of the fourth month, I began my commentary on *The Laṅkāvatāra Sūtra*. There was an extensive famine and, because of a long drought that lasted the whole year, an epidemic broke out, resulting in very many deaths. I was like one sitting in a great cemetery, but I was safe, thanks to the protection given by the power of Dharma. Owing to the drought, all the wells had gone dry. Every night my attendant Fu Shan would wait until midnight to obtain a small tin of water for the following day's

[1] At that time those who were banished had to follow the army which watched them.

use. To the famished people, even a drop was as precious as ambrosia. Corpses were everywhere in and outside the town.

That autumn in the seventh month, I and a scholar, Ko Shih Fu, advised the people to bury putrid corpses and skeletons which numbered about ten thousand. I then held a ceremonial service to pray for rain. On the same day heavy rain fell; the water in the street was three feet deep; and the epidemic was stamped out.

In the eighth month the prefecture ordered me to return to Wu Yang where I stayed at the military training centre and wrote twenty poems about my comings and goings with the army. While on my way to Wu Yang, I passed for the first time through K'u T'eng of Tien Pai district which was the gateway of the country south of Ling Nan. I wrote a literary composition on the occasion and erected a booth to offer free tea to travellers. Imperial counsellor Ting Yu Wu, who had been the victim of a false accusation, was banished to Kuang Hai where I met him and as I had previously held him in high esteem, we became intimate friends.

My fifty-second year (1597–8)
That spring in the first month, there were [again] many deaths and uncovered skeletons in the town [of Wu Yang]. I urged the people to bury them in their thousands. For seven days and nights, I held a ceremony for the welfare of the dead with the help of Ting Yu Wu. From that time the Cantonese who did not know the Buddha began to believe in Him.

That summer in the fourth month, I completed my commentary on *The Laṅkāvatāra Sūtra*. Then because my disciples did not understand the doctrine, I wrote *The Chung Yung Directly Explained* to promote their awakening.[1]

At first, seeing that I was a convicted monk, people despised me. At the time, viceroy Ch'en Ju Kang, minister of war, was very strict in performing his duties; no one dared call on him for private business, so I kept away. However, he diligently sent his men to

---

[1] *The Chung Yung* is one of *The Four Books* of Confucianism. Because Han Shan's disciples were all Confucian, he used that book to explain Buddhism to them.

inquire about me, and in the ninth month, Ting Yu Wu and I called on him together. We were announced by the door-keeper, but I was not received. I then returned. That evening the viceroy came to visit me in a boat bringing food and tea. We sat down and talked until the third night watch. Everyone was astounded. After the visit he praised me in the presence of all the officials, saying: 'He is pre-eminent, above the rest of the Saṅgha.' He then ordered the heads of the three departments[1] to call on me. Since that time the people of the entire Ling Nan region began to respect the Saṅgha.

Commentary by disciple Fu Cheng

Elsewhere master Han Shan recorded:

'When I first called on the viceroy, I had to wait in the court-yard but was not allowed to leave. I thought that I probably was supposed to announce my visit by calling my name [as in the case of those requesting an interview], but felt that I could not do it. However, having no other alternative, I made the effort and called out that I requested an interview. I was not received but was allowed to leave. I did the same thing the next day and received the same treatment. I had this experience for a year, and people said: "How can a military man break a regulation to receive a monk?" Finally when I called again at the viceroy's office, he gave me an appointment and reserved a river boat in which there was a table of vegetarian food and fruits as if a banquet was being given in my honour. I was respectfully invited to take the seat of the distinguished guest. The viceroy said: "I did not mean to be uncompromising with you. Knowing that you have a proud nature, I did it purposely to help you in your achievements." We crossed our legs and had a very friendly chat. I admired him and was surprised that there still existed a man with a mind as profound as his in the higher ranks.'

I heard that when master Han Shan was with the army during his banishment, he took the name of Ts'ai Teh Ch'ing, let his

---

[1] Department of justice, the military, and civil administration.

E

hair and beard grow and wore a Su Tung Po turban; he did this from the age of fifty when he was banished until his sixty-ninth year; he then shaved his hair and beard and again put on the garments of a monk in front of a wooden tablet bearing the name of the deceased empress mother.

My fifty-third year (1598–9)

That spring in the first month, imperial censor Fan Yu Hsien, who had been implicated in the case of the court's saving money for re-building Pao En monastery, was banished to Lei Yang. He called on me at Wu Yang where I was checking the manuscript of my commentary on *The Laṅkāvatāra Sūtra*. When he inquired about the scenery of Lei Yang, I showed him my manuscript, saying: 'This is the scenery of Lei Yang.' He marvelled at my work, praised me, and collected donations for the carving of wooden blocks with which to print it.

Inspector Chou Hai Men, head of Kuang Tung salt tax office, called on me frequently to ask about the Dharma. Because he was at Nan Shao, he requested me to revise *The Ts'ao Ch'i Annals*.[1]

At the time people in Kuang Tung did not know the Buddha. As imperial counsellor Chou Ting Shih was teaching Yang Ming metaphysics, he gathered his followers to question me about Buddhism. A student named Lung Chang wondered at my instruction; after his return he told his friends, Wang An Shun and Feng Ch'ang Li: 'The Ch'an master from the North teaches the Dharma in a very marvellous way.' His two friends came and asked for my instruction. I taught them the transcendental doctrine which they believed and resolved to practise, thanks to their good karmas. The number of those converting to Buddhism gradually increased; from that time the Three Treasures [of Buddha, Dharma and Saṅgha] were well known. These three disciples contributed greatly to the spread of the Dharma.

[1] *The Ts'ao Ch'i Annals* contain the story of the monastery, its rules and regulations set up by various masters, the names of all masters who studied the Dharma and stayed there before and after the Sixth Patriarch, and other similar details.

I had thought of master Ta Kuan's vow to recite *The Lotus Sūtra* to alleviate my suffering and had not been able to requite it. That summer [in order to repay him], I set up a meditation hall inside the fortress[1] where I intended to preach the Dharma with a turban[2] on my head as master Ta Hui had done before me. In order to recite *The Lotus Sūtra* which I expounded to them, I gathered from distant places my old disciples Hsin Yung, Ju Chien and those including Tung An and Ch'ao I who had been ordained under the Bo tree at Fa Hsin monastery, numbering altogether a few tens of persons. When I came to the chapter on 'The Precious Stūpa', I instantly grasped the Buddha's meaning according to which what men see in front of them is but the Pure Land of all the Buddhas. The three transformations mentioned in the sūtra were necessary for those who were of inferior roots. I then wrote a commentary entitled *Applauding the Lotus Sūtra*.

Ting Yu Wu was of a quick and fiery nature, but he was generous. He respected the Saṅgha but did not know the Buddha-Dharma. When I saw him off in a boat, I took advantage of the occasion to put pressure on him and succeeded in helping him to realise his great awakening. I gave him the name of Upāsaka Chiao Fei.[3] I also composed the following gāthā to arouse his alertness on all occasions:

Purify Your Mind

True nature is most profound
Like still and limpid water.
If it is stirred by love and hate,
Passions will arise in waves
The continuance of which
Makes the self-nature turbid;

[1] In China at this time there was in each walled town a small fortress for the protection of its inhabitants against bandits.
[2] In ancient China laymen wore turbans, but monks did not. Tai Hui and Han Shan wore turbans to avoid involving the Saṅgha in their personal troubles.
[3] i.e. 'Aware of Falsehood'.

The troubles of ignorance
All unnoticed will increase.
When selfness clings to otherness,
It is like throwing mud in water.
If otherness stirs selfness,
It is like pouring oil on fire.
When true Self is so disturbed,
Such stirring from an ego comes.
If ego ceases to arise,
Even burning kalpa's icy.[1]
Therefore, a wise man always
Relinquishes his ego.
If there be no ego
All obstructions vanish.
Relinquishment of ego
Depends on long endurance.
When your old habits return,
Be at once on the alert:
Alertness to awareness leads
Which, in a flash, on itself shines back
And sweeps away all traces of them.
At once you will be clear, at ease
In this pure and serene stillness.
Alone and sovereign you will
Enjoy most perfect harmony
Which no externals can equate.

My fifty-fourth year (1599–1600)
In the spring the carving of the wooden blocks for my *Commentary On The Laṅkāvatāra Sūtra* was completed; I took advantage of the occasion to expound the sūtra to my followers. One hundred sets were printed and sent to learned Buddhists in the country and to government officials who were protectors of the Dharma as a means of informing them that although I was in difficulties I had not forgotten the Buddha-work. In case nothing further should be heard

[1] The kalpa of destruction by fire which will turn icy and will not burn you.

of me because of my death, my book would also reveal the nature of my purpose once and for all. However, there were still those who did not believe in me and thought me false.

On the fifteenth day of the seventh month, the Cantonese were accustomed to sacrifice living creatures to their ancestors. On this day the victims were piled up in the market place where they presented a pitiable sight. I therefore organised an Ullambana Meeting[1] at which I gave lectures on filial piety strongly urging my audiences to offer vegetarian meals to Buddhist monks on the day of sacrifice, to free living creatures and to offer only vegetarian food to their ancestors. Those who followed my advice were many, and, since that time, whenever holding funeral ceremonies, observing their parents' birthdays, performing ceremonies to avert calamities, or holding Kṣamayati rites,[2] vegetarian food was offered and living beings were set free. Societies soon sprang up everywhere urging the release of living creatures; these societies helped greatly in converting people to the Buddha-Dharma.

At the time magistrate Yang Fu So, who had been my intimate Dharma-friend, had returned home to mourn for his parents. That autumn I went to visit him, but he had passed away before my arrival. When I was about to return to the mountain the next morning, his body arrived in the town. I went directly to the site of the funeral ceremonies as it was my wish to offer a coffin for the purpose.[3]

As intendant Jen of Shao Yang circuit was also there, he accompanied me to Hui Yang and invited me to visit the West Lake. We climbed White Crane Peak at Tung P'o, and when I left I composed a poem for the occasion. Returning to the place of my abode, I received no visitors to isolate myself for meditation.

---

[1] Festival of All Souls which is held on the 15th day of the seventh month; sūtras are read and offerings made to the Buddhist Trinity for the release from purgatory of the spirits of those who have died either on land or sea.
[2] Confession and asking for pardon.
[3] Yang Fu So left no money for a coffin.

E*

My fifty-fifth year (1600–1)

The entire locality was alarmed by the presence of customs tax collectors. Furthermore, additional alarm was caused by a Japanese invasion so that the whole population was trembling. I scattered my followers and retired to a place of retreat. The Cantonese resented Fukienese white boats which took away their rice, causing prices to soar which led to frequent uprisings. The provincial commander was a Fukienese whose son was aboard a white boat while he himself was about to leave on furlough. The customs collectors took advantage of the situation to create disturbances. When a few white boats appeared they were used to support an allegation that the commander[1] aided his son in the export of rice. Suddenly several thousand persons gathered and began throwing stones at the boat of the commander's son which narrowly escaped being damaged. The rioters surrounded the headquarters and held their weapons ready for an attack. Since all three heads of the provincial administration were at a festival in Tuan Chou, not a single high-ranking official was in town. No aid was forthcoming and the situation appeared to be hopeless. Desperate and unable to do anything, the commander sent his assistant to my place of retreat imploring my help. I declined, saying that I was unable to work miracles. Kneeling and weeping, the officer said: 'You need not think of my chief, but would you neglect to think of the human lives in this locality?' Fearful upon hearing this and feeling the urgent need for something to be done, I ended my retreat, went straight to the customs collectors and urged them to stop the uprising. Since they were prepared to follow my advice, I asked them to quieten and disperse the rioters. Then I went directly to the mob and told them in a loud voice: 'You are causing this disturbance in order to get rice at a low price, but you are breaking the law and inviting the death penalty upon yourselves. If later cheap rice is obtained, who will eat it when you are dead?' The rioters were startled; a moment later, the order [given by the customs collectors] to withdraw arrived; the siege of the headquarters was ended. Conditions returned to normal, and the elders of the town were grateful and thanked me.

[1] This is the same commander who untied the master's rope (see 1596–7).

Meanwhile, the three heads of the provincial administration were dining at Tuan Chou. Hearing of the disturbances, they dropped their chopsticks and left in a hurry. When they returned the town was quiet, but they knew that I had been instrumental in preserving the peace. Intendant Jen heard the news and wrote to me: 'If you had not come out of retreat, how would the locality have fared? Now that you have come out, how will you fare?' I knew myself that I would have no peace [on account of my intervention].

That autumn in the seventh month, intendent Chu Hsing Ts'un of Nan Shao circuit invited me to Ts'ao Ch'i. I took advantage of this and went to the mountain to serve the Sixth Patriarch.

The new viceroy Tai was grateful for my services in connection with the uprising and wanted to see me. He ordered the commander to bring me to his office. When I saw him, I was received with courtesy and given a vegetarian meal. When I called on him before going to Ts'ao Ch'i, he promised to protect the Dharma and told me to report to him whenever necessary. This put my heart at rest.

My fifty-sixth year (1601–2)

That spring in the first month, I arrived at Ts'ao Ch'i only to see that rogues from everywhere had gathered in the monastery where they were slaughtering animals and had opened meat shops. This had been going on for over a century and had resulted in an accumulation of filth and viciousness. The Patriarch's mountain had been invaded by private graves and the Sangha property had been usurped. Moreover, the rogues plotted with villains from outside to intimidate and swindle the monks who dared not even look at them. I sighed and said: 'This is a disease of the internal organs,[1] and if it is not eliminated, the Sixth Patriarch's holy place will become a fox's lair, making the situation hopeless. What shall I do now? There is no way out. What is the use of my staying here?' I pondered over the matter, and, before long, I went to viceroy Tai who said: 'It's simple. I will help you.' He ordered the district magistrate to send guards to the monastery and drive out all the rogues, not

[1] Trouble caused by people inside the monastery which hindered the spreading of the Dharma.

leaving one behind and destroying all the meat shops in three days.

From then on the monastery of Ts'ao Ch'i was cleansed of all the accumulated filth. The viceroy served me a vegetarian meal and during our conversation, he said: 'I have cleansed the Sixth Patriarch's monastery of all that dirt for you. At present ruin is coming to the people. Great Bodhisattva, please have mercy on them. What will you do to save them?' I asked him: 'What is the trouble?' He replied: 'There are a thousand boats belonging to pearl divers who are notorious bandits and are taking advantage of an imperial order to dive for pearls by refusing to return to their native places even when their work is finished. They are causing mischief at sea, plundering wherever they go. The law cannot stop them. This is one thing, another is that mines are being opened and the miners are being oppressive and unreasonable. Graves are dug up and property's destroyed; everywhere people are the victims of this havoc which is worse than the piracy. They cannot live in peace. What can be done?' I said: 'This isn't an easy matter. We must consider it carefully.'

It so happened that Li, the officer in charge of the pearl fishery and the mining, was a Buddhist devotee. That autumn he came to Ts'ao Ch'i to pay reverence to the Sixth Patriarch and stayed at the monastery for a few days, listening with great delight to the Dharma. I took the opportunity to urge him to give a donation for the rehabilitation of the monastery and he responded warmheartedly. I then told him in secret: 'The pearl fishery and mining activities are playing havoc in the country; this is certainly not the emperor's will. A time limit should be set within which the boats must disperse, a penalty being imposed for failure to do so. The mining should be stopped and the miners withdrawn. A yearly remittance [to the central authorities] should be made by the department of mines, which should not allow the inhabitants to be molested because of its activities. Can all this be done?' He promised to act and peace returned to the sea and the mountain regions.

The viceroy was deeply moved, and to thank me wrote: 'Now I realise the immense compassion of the Buddha and Patriarchs.' He became an enthusiastic protector of the Dharma, and my mind was put at ease at Ts'ao Ch'i. I then extended the monastery, improved the roads, selected monks to teach the precepts, opened free schools to train young monks, appointed a treasurer, laid down rules, investigated rents and taxes, redeemed the monastery's properties, and returned those that had been usurped from outside. All this was accomplished in a single year.

My fifty-seventh year (1602–3)
That year the Sixth Patriarch's hall was repaired. The ground behind it was banked up with earth and the paths and lanes were improved. The meat shops were converted into dwellings for monks coming from the ten directions. I exposed heterodoxy, moved the dormitory, opened the meditation hall and made regulations for observance.

My fifty-eighth year (1603–4)
That winter in the eleventh month, master Ta Kuan, who was in the capital, was put into prison following receipt by the government of an anonymous letter. At the trial he was found to be involved in my case. I knew I could not escape the consequences, but put my mind at ease and waited for the result. Thanks to the emperor's clemency, I was [spared and] allowed to travel to the South.

Commentary by disciple Fu Cheng

That year master Ta Kuan passed away in prison, but [master] Han Shan's autobiography does not mention the cause of death. The following passages are from master Han Shan's *Journey to the East* which contains an inscription composed by him for the tablet of the stūpa erected for master Ta Kuan and other records [relating to his Dharma-friend]. The inscription for the tablet reads:

'The master's name was Chen K'o and his aliases were Ta Kuan and Tsu Pai; he was called "The Honoured One" by his followers in reverence for the Dharma. His lay surname was Ch'en. His

father was a native of Chu Ch'u but moved to the shore of Tai
Wu lake in Wu Chiang district. Until the age of five, he could
not speak. One day a monk passed by the door, touched the
child's head and told the father: "This boy will leave home and
become a master of men and devas." After saying this, the monk
disappeared. The master then could speak. In his youth he was of
a generous and forceful character; so that women did not dare
approach him. When he was seventeen, he longed to travel in the
North armed with a sword. On his arrival at the Chang Men gate
of the walled town of Su Chou [Soochow], he was caught in
heavy rain. Bhikṣu Ming Chiao of Hu Chiu monastery saw him
and wondered at his distinguished features which surpassed those
common for his age. The bhikṣu shared his umbrella with him
and, after their arrival at the monastery, offered him food and
lodging. That night master Ta Kuan heard the monks reciting
The Sūtra of Eighty-eight Buddhas' Names; at daybreak he took ten
gold coins from his belt and offered them to the bhikṣu, requesting to have his head shaved and to be allowed to accept him as
his master. He came and went frequently in the San Wu region.

'One day he left bhikṣu Ming Chiao. When he heard a monk
recite Chang Chue's gāthā "Perceiving Truth", a great feeling of
doubt surged in his mind as the monk came to the following
lines:

"To stop wrong thinking aggravates the illness
But to seek the absolute is also wrong."

Wherever he went he wrote this verse on the wall, doubting
again and again until his head became swollen. One day while
taking his vegetarian meal, he attained sudden self-realisation and
the swelling disappeared completely. After that he called on
many learned masters, passed through Kuang Shan, and plunged
into study of the teaching of the Dharmalakṣaṇa school.[1] One day
after walking twenty [Chinese] miles, his feet became sore, so he
tied stone [tablets] under them until he could walk two hundred
miles a day, and then he stopped using them. He visited Five

[1] Dharmalakṣaṇa are the aspects and characteristics of things.

Peak Mountain and went to the capital where he called on the aged master Pien Yung who kept him as a guest monk. He then called on such learned masters as Hisao Yen, Hsien Li and others. He saw master Ta Chien Jun who was talking about Kung Ans, about the use of the mouth and ear for sealing the mind and of handkerchiefs for its transmission. He sighed [at hearing such heretical talk] and said: "Is this the purpose of [Bodhidharma's] coming from the West?" He did not join the audience.

'He went to the South where he had a disciple, bhikṣu Tao K'ai of Mi Ts'ang monastery at Chia Ho, a native of Nan Ch'ang and a scholar who had left home to become a monk. In the town was Leng Yen monastery, now in ruins, where master Chang Shui once wrote commentaries on the sūtras. Master Ta Kuan and minister Lu Wu T'ai agreed to restore the splendour of Chang Shui's teaching and thus undertook to rebuild a five-pillared Ch'an hall. When it was completed, the master cut his arm with an awl and with a bowlful of his blood wrote two scrolls as follows:

"If the mind is not looked into, meditation increases karmic suffering."

"If thinking is well guarded, even offending Buddhas will help right practice."

'He thought of the bulky, cumbersome volumes of *The Tripiṭaka* which [because of the difficulty in circulating them] deprived distant and isolated regions of the Buddha-Dharma; he wished to publish them in handy, rectangular books for easy circulation that could be made available everywhere and, thus, sow the Diamond seeds. He was ready to assume full responsibility if such a plan were criticised. He spoke of his intention and after deliberation minister Lu, imperial tutor Feng Meng Chen, chief justic Tseng Tung Meng, and lord high chamberlain Ch'u Ju Chi collected workmen at Chi Chao monastery on Ching Shan Mountain, putting bhikṣus Tao K'ai of Mi Ts'ang, Pen of Huan Yu, and K'ai of Tan Ch'u in charge of the work. Later financial commissioner Wu Yung Hsien of T'ung Ch'eng rehabilitated

Hua Cheng temple as a place for storing the wooden printing blocks.

'As the carving of wooden blocks for printing *The Tripiṭaka* was now decided upon at Chia Ho, master Ta Kuan returned to Wu Men to visit his master Ming Chiao who had returned to lay life and was a physician. When the latter saw his former disciple, he was taken by surprise. Master Ta Kuan wept and urged Ming Chiao to shave his head. Gradually convinced, Ming Chiao became the master's disciple.

'At this time seniors of the Chen and Chou clans of the Wu Chiang region, of the Ho and Sun clans of Ch'u A district, and of the Yu and Wang clans of Chin Sha district, led their clansmen to pay reverence to master Ta Kuan and to follow him.

'In Yu Yuan garden he copied out *The Lotus Sūtra* to pay the debt of gratitude that he owed his parents. Hearing that Miao Feng was erecting an iron stūpa in Lu Ya monastery, he sent his copy of the sūtra to be put inside it.

'Master Ta Kuan came to see me at Tung Hai; but since I had gone to the capital to express my gratitude to the empress mother [for her donation of *The Tripiṭaka*], he took bhikṣu Tao K'ai with him and came to Chiao Hai River which was swollen by autumn floods. It was generally believed that it could not be crossed, but he took off his robe and waded in. When he was up to his shoulders, he called back to the others to follow. After having crossed, he said: "In a life and death crisis, one must cross over straightforwardly in order to get through."[1]

'When I was in the capital, I heard from his disciple Yu Yu that he was going to the East. I packed in a hurry, made forced marches day and night, also crossed the river that was flowing out of its accustomed channel, and hurried to Chi Mo. He was leaving the mountain and when we met, we were greatly delighted, returning to the mountain together where he stayed for ten days. We thus satisfied the greatest desire of our lives.

[1] Referring to those who wish to ferry themselves to the other shore or Enlightenment.

'Master Ta Kuan returned to the capital, restored the ancient Tan Che monastery and from San Chin, passed through Kuan Chung and walked on paths [made with planks] in steep places. Finally he reached Sze Chuan province where he visited Mount O Mei and paid his reverence to Samantabhadra Bodhisattva....[1] As upāsaka Yuan Tzu Hua asked to be made a monk, master Ta Kuan shaved his head on the mountain and gave him the Dharma name of Fa K'ai [Dharma Armour].

'He stopped there for a rest before resuming his journey to the North. He arrived at the grotto of Stone Sūtras and restored Dharma-master Ching Wan's stūpa and temple. When the grotto was opened, he found a container of relics which emitted rays that lighted the dark [interior of the] grotto. The empress mother heard of this and sent him a purple robe as a gift and money to purchase offerings to the relics in the grotto.

'Hearing that he was journeying in the West, I hurried to the capital and waited for him at Tusiṭa monastery. When he saw me he took me by the hand and together we visited the Stone Sūtra grotto where I wrote The Story of the Grotto. We left the mountain and stayed at a garden in the western suburb of the town. There we sat [with crossed legs] face to face for forty successive days and nights during which we did not sleep a wink. This was the most wonderful time of my life.

'When master Ta Kuan was at Tan Che, he vowed not to take his meals before paying reverence to the Buddha. One day while receiving visitors, he inadvertently ate before paying reverence. He ordered the monastery's director of affairs [karmadāna] to give him thirty strokes of the staff. He lay face down before the Buddha shrine and received the beating which blackened both his thighs. Afterward he said: "Since time without beginning, the power of habit over living beings is like oil that has been absorbed by flour and cannot be uprooted. If no pain is inflicted, the power of habit cannot be conquered."

'In my fiftieth year, he was at Kuang Shan and ready to pro-

[1] An assistant of the Buddha; he is often seen in Buddhist art riding a white elephant.

ceed to the capital to rescue me when he heard that I was being banished to the South. Waiting on the river bank, he met me, at Lu Po temple at Hsia Kuan. Taking my hand he sighed and said: "You face death to continue the Dharma work. The ancients who sacrificed everything for the Dharma had the determination of Ch'eng Ying Kung and Sun Ch'u Chiu. I am just small fry, but if you don't return alive, it will mean my end." I repeatedly consoled him; and, as we were about to part company, he said: "I will die before you, leaving everything in your hands." So we departed forever.

'Five years after I crossed the Ta Yu range, he sighed because I did not wear the monk's robe and said: "Thus there is no one [competent] at the Dharma-door [to Enlightenment]. If we sit and watch the destruction of the Dharma-standard, to what will those who want to perpetuate and prosper the Three Treasures [of Buddha, Dharma and Saṅgha] apply their minds? If master Han Shan does not return, there will be a great hindrance to the aim that caused me to leave the world to become a monk. If the mining tax is not abolished, it will be a great handicap to the fulfilment of my vow to save the world. As long as the Transmission of the Lamp is not continued, my realisation of wisdom [Prajñā] will be greatly hindered. If I am relieved of these three handicaps, I will make no more journeys to the capital."

'In my fifty-eighth year, I was at Ts'ao Ch'i and wrote a letter delivered by my disciple Ch'i Chieh, inviting him to come to the mountain [and stay with me]. . . . Suddenly the whole country was shaken by the story of a strange letter [accusing people of plotting to kill the heir to the throne], and those who hated him presented a petition of accusation against him. Thus, his misfortune arose. Earlier the emperor had copied out *The Diamond Sūtra* and inadvertently stained it with his own perspiration. As he did not know whether he could change the paper or not, he sent a messenger seeking master Ta Kuan's advice. In reply, the latter presented the sovereign with the following gāthā:

> "Your majesty, one drop of your sweat
> Serves as a bridge for generations;
> The Dharma-store that has no end
> Will henceforth emit rays of light."

The emperor read the gāthā and was extremely pleased. When the accusation reached him, he merely ordered an investigation, but when the chief of the imperial guards questioned master Ta Kuan, he would only talk about the three handicaps [referred to above]. Imperial censor Ts'ao Hsueh Ch'eng visited him in prison, inquired about the Dharma and compiled the master's *Sayings in Prison*.

'At the time a government official intended to put the master to death. Hearing this Ta Kuan said: "This world-dharma being such as it is, what is the use of my remaining any longer?" He took a bath, sat erect, chanted a gāthā and passed away. When imperial censor Ts'ao heard of the master's death, he hurried to the prison, patted the body and said: "Your leave is well taken!" Thereupon, master Ta Kuan opened his eyes, smiled and departed. He passed away at the age of sixty-one, his Dharma-age being forty.'

I heard the following story about master Ta Kuan:

'When the crown prince was proclaimed heir to the throne, someone sent an anonymous letter to the chief minister of state alleging that the mother of prince Fu was plotting to kill the heir. When the emperor heard of this, he was very angry and ordered that the culprits be found and arrested. Innocent people were involved in the criminal charge, and even premier Ch'en Li and minister of rites Kuo Cheng Yu narrowly escaped misfortune.'

The *Story of Master Ta Kuan* relates:

'At the interrogation, the chief of the imperial guards shouted: "You should know who sent that anonymous letter." The master replied: "I do not know anything about it." The chief retorted: "Why don't you know?" The master replied: "I am a monk and know nothing about it." When questioned further, he enumerated the three handicaps, adding nothing else.

'One day before his death, he wrote a letter to Lu Tan Yuan, minister Lu Wu T'ai's son, who was at Shui Ts'ao at the time. The letter said: "It is very dark here. Please buy and send me immediately seven crystal lamps so that I can perform the rite to bring about the unsurpassed brightness." Lu Tan Yuan complied and sent the lamps to the prison. The next day the master put the lamps on a stand, lit them, sat erect and sang the following gāthā:

> "A smile comes not without a special cause.
> Who knows that Nothingness contains no dust?[1]
> Henceforth I tuck up the feet my mother gave me;[2]
> The iron tree waits not for the spring to blossom." [3]

My fifty-ninth year (1604–5)

That spring in the first month, an order was given to the provincial court to return me to the place of my banishment because of master Ta Kuan's case. I left Ts'ao Ch'i and went back to Lei Chou as ordered. I recalled that master Ta Kuan had once said: 'The Śūraṅgama Sūtra deals with cause and effect in the seven states [gatis][4] but there are no worldly classics that explain them.' I rememered my reply: 'The Spring and Autumn Annals indicate clearly the law of cause and effect.' I then wrote my book Tso Chiu Ming's Doctrine of the Mind in The Spring and Autumn Annals.[5]

My sixtieth year (1605–6)

That spring in the third month, I crossed the Hai Nan sea and

[1] The purity of the self-nature cannot be mixed with worldly things.
[2] The self-natured Dharmakāya has its substance and function. 'Tucking up the feet' represents the return of function to substance and 'stretching out the feet' represents its function.
[3] 'The iron tree in blossom' stands for the mind stripped of all worldly attachments and ready to attain Enlightenment.
[4] Gati, the seven states of living beings: hell, hungry ghost, animal, man, seer (ṛṣi), deva and asura.
[5] Han Shan wrote the book as an indirect warning to the ruling emperor about the harmful effects of former emperors' blind confidence in their concubines which was the cause of the fall of certain dynasties.

visited Kuang Lang temple of poet Su Tung P'o and White Dragon spring. I found no trace of the former monastery of Ch'an master Chiao Fan. I stayed at Ming Chang monastery and wrote the preface to my book *Tso Chiu Ming's Doctrine of the Mind in The Spring and Autumn Annals.* I journeyed to Shih Shan Mountain and wrote my *Exploration in Hai Nan Sea* and *The Gold Corn Fountain.*

At night I went to the top of the wall of the town of Wen Chang which appeared spiritless and deserted except for the western suburb where there were signs of life. I informed my followers: 'This town is on the brink of disaster; you must hasten to pray that it be averted.' People thought I was being absurd; but a fortnight after my departure, a violent earthquake destroyed every one of the official buildings in the eastern area as well as the town's wall and gate. The stūpa of Ming Chang monastery collapsed and crushed the house where I would have been staying.

Earlier as I was leaving Wen Chang, the people did their utmost to keep me but I declined. If I had remained, I would have been smashed to bits. After the disaster they marvelled at my prediction.

When I left and recrossed Hai Nan sea, it was a moonlight night and I could see the beautiful scenery of Hai Nan Island. It is one of the ten great islands and to my eyes looked like a home for immortals.

That summer in the fourth month, the viceroy ordered me to return to Wu Yang. In the seventh month of that autumn, I went to Ts'ao Ch'i to complete the rebuilding of the Sixth Patriarch's monastery. When I left, the monastery had already been pulled down and was being rebuilt; now upon my arrival, about sixty to seventy per cent of the work had been completed. As there was no money to meet the cost of materials and labour amounting to one thousand gold coins, I urged two court officials to give donations which were used to pay the debt and also to rehabilitate Chang Ch'un temple at Wu Yang which was to be used as an office for the reconstruction of the Sixth Patriarch's monastery.

My sixty-first year (1606–7)
That spring in the third month, I crossed Ta Yu Mountain and

visited Ting Yu Wu at Nan Chou. I called on premier Chang Hung
Yang who had been chief minister of state when I was arrested and
knew all about my case. He had striven to rescue me and I was
grateful to him, so as he was now in retirement and living at home,
I went to thank him. He was very happy to see me and gathered my
followers for a vegetarian meal with me at Hsien Yun restaurant.
During the meal he said: 'Everybody knows that master Han Shan
is a learned master, but no one knows that he has achieved secret
merits for the dynasty.'[1] Hearing this, those present were taken
aback. They asked him to elucidate and he did so. The appearance
of the entire gathering was completely transformed. On that
occasion I composed six poems. ·

Then I returned to Ts'ao Ch'i and passed through Wen Chiang
where I called on imperial counsellor Chou who invited me to stay
with him for a few days. I went to Chang Kung where general
Ch'en Erh Shih kept me at his headquarters. There I fell ill for a
month during which I wrote twelve poems. I then returned to
Ts'ao Ch'i.

That autumn in the eighth month, the emperor's grandson was
born, and an amnesty was extended to old and sick prisoners in
banishment and to those wrongly banished who could appeal for
redress and release. As I was entitled to the benefit, I presented myself at the headquarters of the commander-in-chief who granted my
appeal and transmitted it to the local authorities at Lei Chou where
it was determined that my case was covered by the amnesty. The
provincial judge released me and thus I left the army.

My sixty-second year (1607–8)
That spring in the third month, I asked for leave to return to my
native place, but the viceroy's office instead issued orders to Shao
Yang prefecture to arrange for me to remain at Ts'ao Ch'i. During
my stay in the mountain, I taught the Buddha-Dharma to my
followers.

When I was young, I had read Lao Tzu's *Tao Teh Ching* which is

[1] This refers to changing the Mokṣa-pariṣad meeting to a prayer meeting for
the protection of the imperial rule and the birth of the heir to the throne.

an ancient classic of profound meaning and very difficult to understand. I had studied it eagerly and already understood it. Because my
lay followers had once requested me to write a commentary on the
book, I gave it thought and began it at the age of forty-seven. Each
time I wrote something, I did it only after a thorough examination
of the text. If I was in doubt about a single character, I did not let
it pass. I had worked hard on the book for the last fifteen years,
carrying it with me wherever I went. It is only now that the
commentary is completed.

Commentary by disciple Fu Cheng

Master Han Shan wrote elsewhere:
   'My *Commentary on the Tao Teh Ching* was put into manuscript
form thirteen years after I had conceived the idea of writing it.
The meaning of the book can be grasped only after one has had a
personal experience of it. It cannot be said that words on paper
have no real flavour.

   'When writing a commentary on a sūtra, I would make a
mental concentration in order to see into it and be in accord with
the Buddha-mind. By so doing, the clue to the correct meaning
would jump out instantly and I would write it down on paper.
If the thinking process were involved, it would not serve the
purpose.'

My sixty-third year (1608–9)
It was decided to repair the great hall of Ts'ao Ch'i monastery. That
spring in the second month, intendant Feng Yuan Cheng of the
western circuit, who was a native of Chiang Su [Kiangsu] province,
came to see me on the mountain [at Ts'ao Ch'i]. He spent the night
in the monastery and saw the Bodhisattva in a dream. Impressed by
the apparition, he entered the hall the next morning to pay reverence to the Buddha. Reaching the shrine of the Three Holy Ones
[of the Western Paradise], he saw two worn pillars and was taken
aback; he told me: 'Why don't you repair them?' I replied: 'The
amount of money involved is large and far exceeds our means.'

'How much?' he asked. When I gave him an idea of the sum, he said: 'This is not difficult; I will try to get the money.' After his return, he reported the matter to viceroy Tai who said: 'Perilous indeed! When one sees a child fall into a well, one crawls down to save him. Now that the holy site of Buddhas and Bodhisattvas is endangered, one cannot be called a gentleman if one remains unmoved.' He inquired about the cost and intendant Feng mentioned the amount. The viceroy said: 'Perhaps this is not sufficient.' He then ordered the Nan Shao circuit to send an official to make an estimate on the spot, consulting me for the purpose. Later I went to see him; because he intended to provide the money himself, I said: 'It would be inconvenient to use public money for this purpose. It will be all right if the Dharma-door's established precedent is followed.'[1] He asked: 'What shall I do?' I proposed that subscriptions be collected and that instructions be given to the western circuit to prepare twelve subscription books, one for each department, inviting donations; all subscriptions collected this way would be sent directly to the viceroy's office and not to the monks. This proposal would be easy to carry out. The viceroy agreed, and, within a month, a total of nearly one thousand gold pieces was obtained. I went personally to buy timber in the western region. When I reached Tuan Chou, I was detained there by the viceroy to supervise repairs to Pao Yueh hall; another official was ordered to buy the timber. That winter the repairs were completed and I wrote the story of the hall. All the timber that had been bought was on the bank and was gradually being sent down the river.

In the eleventh month of that winter, bandits from Indochina broke into the Ch'in Chou district. As viceroy Tai petitioned for a military expedition against them, an inquiry was ordered which resulted in his being dismissed from his high position.

---

[1] The 'established precedent' was that when a monastery was in need of funds, monks were sent to towns and cities to ask people for money; the names of donors and the amounts were recorded in 'subscription books'.

Commentary by disciple Fu Cheng

Viceroy Tai was head of Kuang Tung province for nine years, during which he dealt easily—thanks to master Han Shan's help —with a number of uprisings by insurgents. This is why the viceroy gave his valuable support to rehabilitate the Sixth Patriarch's monastery. As for the great hall, it was decided to use for the pillars and beams hard wood the purchase and transportation of which from West Kuang Tung cost three thousand gold pieces. If the viceroy had remained in office for another year, the reconstruction of Ts'ao Ch'i monastery would have been more satisfactorily completed.

Before his dismissal the viceroy used the master to supervise repairs to Pao Yueh hall. At the time tribes from Indochina broke into Ch'in Chou and defeated the local authorities. The emperor heard of this and the viceroy narrowly escaped being apprehended [by the central government]. Master Han Shan used his good name to come personally with the monastery's banner to the cave where the chief of the tribes stayed to urge him to surrender. Following their withdrawal, peace and order returned, saving the entire Ch'in Chou region which had a population of one million.

Viceroy Tai then petitioned for an expedition against the invaders in order to conceal the defeat of the local authorities, and this is why he was only dismissed and was not apprehended as well. Master Han Shan's intervention was also a valuable repayment for the help that had been given by the viceroy to rehabilitate the monastery at Ts'ao Ch'i. However, the master did not mention either his service or the viceroy's fault.

My sixty-fourth year (1609-10)
That spring in the second month, I left Tuan Chou [by boat] with a cargo of timber, but because of adverse winds I stopped at Ling Yang pass. I took the opportunity to visit Tuan Ch'i and wrote *A Dreamy Journey to Tuan Ch'i*. When the timber reached Meng Chiang, I went to the mountain to collect men to unload it. How-

ever, there were a few degenerate monks who opposed me and incited the men to cause trouble as if they were rioters. Seeing all this, I sighed and said: 'This is because of my deviation from the Buddha-Dharma through wrong attachments to externals.' While the men were starting to cause trouble, I took a seat in the hall, burned incense sticks and recited *The Diamond Sūtra*. When I came to the Buddha's expounding of 'Four views which really were not four views', I achieved a major awakening. Then I wrote *The Diamond Cutter of Doubts*.[1] When the manuscript was finished, all the men remained silent. Those degenerate monks, who did not believe me and were seduced into error by scoundrels, were fearful and brought the case before a court. I appeared before it and then awaited its decision staying in a boat on Fu Jung River for two years and spending all my travelling expenses. At the time, subprefect Hsiang Ch'u Tung, who was guardian of the gates at Han Chiang, invited me to come and see him. I took a boat which was subsequently destroyed in a gale. When I arrived, I became gravely ill and was saved from death by a physician who was summoned by the subprefect. When I returned to the district, I was sick for nearly a year in a hotel.

My sixty-fifth year (1610–11)
That year I lived in a boat on the river. In the seventh month of that autumn, the criminal investigation official arrived in the district and called on me. Only after the official's arrival did the judge begin to examine the case and find me guilty. The official rejected the judge's decision and said: 'The master has rendered a great service to the Sixth Patriarch and all that he handed over to the monastery will now benefit those degenerate monks. If he is now found guilty, can this be called equality or justice as taught by the Buddha?' The circuit administrator was again ordered to make a thorough investigation of the case. Consequently, the administrator himself went to the mountain, examined carefully item by item the accusations that had been made by the degenerate monks and discovered

[1] Cf *Ch'an and Zen Teaching, First Series, The Diamond Cutter of Doubts*. Rider, London.

them to be completely unfounded. They had accused me of embezzling over eight thousand gold pieces. However, when I made the rules for the monastery's finances, I had introduced a voucher system. All the receipts and disbursements had been supervised by the secretary and were accompanied by numbered vouchers. It was discovered that I had never touched the monastery's funds. . . . Thus everyone in and outside the monastery realised that I was not in the wrong. As the matter was now clear, the authorities were very angry with those monks, and I did my best to help them. I was asked repeatedly to stay at the mountain, but feeling tired I declined. I gave the direction of the monastery to my disciple bhikṣu Huai Yu and departed.

My sixty-sixth year (1611–12)
That spring in the third month, I convalesced on Ting Wu mountain in Tuan Chou district.

When I was paroled following the amnesty, I waited for the required formalities to be completed. Because nothing was heard from the criminal investigation authorities, my case was kept in abeyance. Another inquiry was held to make my release official. I was then free to move as I liked.

My followers asking for my instruction, I wrote my *Elucidating Doubts About The Great Learning*.[1]

My sixty-seventh year (1612–13)
I stayed at Chang Ch'un temple where at my followers' request I gave lectures on *The Śraddhotpāda Śāstra* [The Awakening of Faith], the *Eight Parijñānas*[2] and the *Hundred Divisions*.[3] Because my commentary *Applauding The Lotus Sūtra* was not divided into chapters to tally exactly with the text of the sūtra and therefore caused my

[1] *The Great Learning* is one of *The Four Books* of Confucianism.
[2] The eight consciousnesses.
[3] The Hundred Divisions of all mental qualities and their agents, according to the Dharmalakṣaṇa school: (1) the eight perceptions of forms of consciousness; (2) the fifty-one mental ideas; (3) the five physical organs and their six modes of sense; (4) twenty-four indefinites or unconditioned elements; (5) six inactive metaphysical concepts.

students difficulty, I wrote another book entitled *A Commentary On The Lotus Sūtra, Chapter by Chapter.*

My sixty-eighth year (1613-14)

I ended the summer retreat for my disciples at Chang Ch'un temple where I lectured on *The Sūtra of Complete Enlightenment.*[1] When I had finished half my lectures, there appeared on my back a huge abscess for which medicine was of no avail. My end seeming almost certain, commander Wang Han Ch'ung made the necessary preparations for my death.

It happened that at the time a Cantonese named Liang Hsing Shan, a drinker of strong wines and a specialist in the treatment of ulcers, arrived unexpectedly at the temple. He examined my abscess and said: 'It is indeed serious! Any further delay will be fatal. But don't worry, you will be all right.' He used herbs which were [crushed and] applied on the abscess, giving as if by magic instant relief. It was completely healed that winter and I wrote a literary composition thanking the physician.

I had had a similar abscess previously [at the age of twenty-one] when I sat in meditation in the beginning [of my Ch'an practice]. I knew it was a karmic debt, and at that time I recited *The Avataṁsaka Sūtra* asking for respite [to complete my meditations]. Thereafter, whenever I recited or copied that sūtra, the abscess appeared again and vanished after I said prayers. When I was in Kuang Tung province, it reappeared twice but harmlessly. The disease was in my body for forty-eight years. This time when it first returned, I paid no attention and did not even know that it was an abscess. Subsequently it became a serious matter. Thus I had a personal experience of the settlement of a karmic debt, clear proof of the infallibility of karma.

In the tenth month I got rid of the abscess. Originally the chief of rites Tseng Chin Chien, who was a friend of mine, had had an understanding with me that we were going to pass our old age together at Nan Yo. He wrote over ten letters to me about the matter,

[1] Cf *Ch'an and Zen Teaching, Third Series, Part III—The Sūtra of Complete Enlightenment.* Rider, London.

but I could not carry it out. Now he wrote me again and sent my disciple Hsuan Chan to welcome me. So I took my staff, left Kuang Tung and went there [to Nan Yo].

When I first came to Kuang Tung province, my disciples at Fa Hsing monastery numbered several tens. Gradually they dispersed and there remained only bhikṣus Tung Chiung and Ch'ao I, who in my illness and misfortune did not forsake me; there also was Tung An who came and went frequently. When I left, they did not let me go alone. Tung An and Chao I carried a large umbrella and followed me. I took with me my attendants Fu Hai, Kuang I and Kuang Cheng. We crossed the peak and in the eleventh month arrived at Hu Tung where I stayed. My disciple Fu Shan and my attendant Shen Kuang, who had visited their parents in the North, rejoined me a few days later.

My sixty-ninth year (1614–15)
My disciples, who were unable to follow me when I left Kuang Tung province, were thinking of me [while I was away] and their esteem for me increased. My follower Feng Ch'i Nan and other disciples sent a letter inviting Fu Hui to take the seat which I had left vacant. That year I sent Fu Shan to accompany Fu Hui who returned to Kuang Tung.

Toward the end of that spring, I visited Teh Shan Mountain to pay reverence to master Teh Shan and wrote four poems on the occasion. I visited upāsaka Feng Yuan Cheng at Wu Ling where I composed two poems and met attendant Lung. At Chu Ling I accepted prince Yung's offering of vegetarian food, while at Ta Shan temple the monks invited me to give lectures on the Buddhist precepts. Upāsaka Feng and his friends gave donations for the rehabilitation of T'an Hua vihāra. On my return to Heng Yang, my boat passed through Hsiang Tan where I met upāsaka Pai I Fu.

In the fourth month of that summer, I returned to Hu Kuang where I learned of the death of the empress mother. I held a funeral ceremony to repay the debt of gratitude that I owed her; an imperial proclamation was issued for the ceremony. Before the

F

tablet [bearing the empress mother's name], I shaved my hair and beard and once again wore the monk's robe.

Ever since my stay at Tung Hai, I had been planning to write a commentary entitled *A Thorough Explanation of The Śūraṅgama Sūtra*,[1] but although I had kept the idea in mind I had had no time to do it. In the fifth month of that summer, I began to write and completed it in fifty days.

In the eleventh month T'uan Hua vihāra was repaired and I composed a poem on my stay in the mountain. At the time my disciples Wu Hsin and Chuan Yu came to see me.

My seventieth year (1615–16)
That spring I gave lectures on my *Commentary on The Śūraṅgama Sūtra*.

In the fourth month of that summer, I wrote *A Thorough Explanation of The Lotus Sūtra*. Although I had already written two short commentaries on that sūtra, they did not tally with the text and were not thoroughly explanatory. This is why I wrote a third [more detailed] commentary which (like the one I wrote on *The Śūraṅgama Sūtra*) was also completed in fifty days. I lectured on *The Awakening of Faith* and wrote a commentary on it.

In the seventh month of that autumn, I visited Nan Yo Mountain and climbed Chu Yung peak where I wrote a poem. On the double-nine festival,[2] upāsaka Feng Yuan Cheng, who had been transferred from Wu.Ling to the command of Hu Nan, invited me to visit Fang Kuang with him. After his return to town, he and inspector Wu Sheng Pai came to see me at Hu Tung. Inspector Wu was very pleased when we talked about my *Commentary on The Śūraṅgama Sūtra*. He and his subordinates gave a donation to pay for carving wooden blocks to print it. We paid reverence to a picture of the eighty-eight ancestors[3] which the inspector greatly

[1] Cf *The Śūraṅgama Sūtra*, translated by Charles Luk. Rider, London, 1965.
[2] The ninth day of the ninth month.
[3] Fifty-three Buddhas who are listed in *The Sūtra of Bhaiṣajya-samudgata Bodhisattva and Bhaiṣajya-rāja Bodhisattva* and thirty-five Buddhas listed in *The Mahāratnakūṭa Sūtra*.

THE AUTOBIOGRAPHY OF CH'AN MASTER HAN SHAN   145

admired. He ordered an artist to copy it in an album in which he asked me to write an eulogy for each ancestor. Soon after he had settled in his post, upāsaka Feng invited me to visit Chiu I Mountain.

In the tenth month, I proceeded to the Ling Ling district where I passed the winter at Yu Ch'i.

My seventy-first year (1616–17)

That spring in the first month, I returned from Ling Ling. A year after the death of Ch'an master Ta Kuan, my disciple Ta I had brought the coffin south where it was enshrined at Chi Chao monastery on Chin Shan Mountain for worship by his followers, monks and laymen alike. Twelve years had now elapsed and it was impossible for me to forget my loyalty to this Dharma-friend. I had longed to go there personally to present my condolence, but had not even sent incense sticks. Hearing of the date of burial, I wanted to be present for the occasion. Since I also had an invitation to go to Tung Ch'an monastery at Chin Sha, I took advantage of it to make the journey. When I was about to leave, I was invited to a vegetarian dinner that was given by the monks of Hua Yao monastery on the occasion of a successional ceremony. I passed Mei Hsueh hall where I paid my condolatory reverence to Ch'an master Hsun An.

That summer in the fourth month, I left Hu Tung and composed a poem entitled 'A Trip to Nan Yo to Stop the Jeering'. On the fifth day of the fifth month, I arrived at Wu Chang where I paid reverence to the great statue of Buddha. I visited Chiu Feng and paid reverence to Ch'an master Wu Nien's stūpa. In the sixth month I arrived at Hsun Yang and visited Tung Ling monastery where I wrote a poem entitled 'In Remembrance of the Ancients'. I climbed Kuang Lu Mountain and presented my condolence to the late master Ch'e K'ung. To escape the heat of summer, I stayed in the Chin Chu plateau where I wrote my *Commentary on Chao Lun*. I found the site secluded and to my liking and planned to make a place of retirement there. I also visited places noted for scenery.

In the seventh month, I visited Kuei Tsung and climbed Gold Wheel peak where I paid reverence to the Śarīra Stūpa and wrote a

poem for the occasion. At the same time a monk offered me Wu
Ju hall as a place of retreat, and after I had climbed to see the site
which although not large was very lonely, I accepted the offer. At
the time a scholar named Hsing Lai Tzu wanted to be an almsgiver
and offered fifty gold pieces to buy the mountain for me in order
that I might satisfy my desire to spend my old age there. Hearing of
my arrival, adviser Ch'en Ch'ih Shih of Fou Liang also came to see
me. He took a vow to act as Dharma-protector when he heard of
my intention to stay at Kuang Shan Mountain.

In the eighth month of that autumn, I left the mountain and
arrived at Huang Mei where I paid reverence to the Fourth and
Fifth Ch'an Patriarchs and visited subprefect Wang. I went to Tzu
Yun Shan Mountain and stayed there for ten days. Subprefect
Wang offered money to build a vihāra on Kuang Shan Mountain
for me and invited prince Ching, envoy Yuan and others to form a
Society of Seven Wise Men. I left the place and proceeded to T'ung
Ch'eng where I called on academician Wu Kuan Wo and magistrate Wu Pen Ju who wanted to build a monastery for my retire-
ment. I visited Fou Shan, wrote a poem and crossed the river to
climb Chiu Hua Mountain.

At the beginning of the tenth month, I arrived at Tung Ch'an
monastery at Ching Sha where I met upāsakas Yu, Wang and Sun.
Then I left Chin Sha and went to Shuang Ching Mountain. I passed
Ch'u A where magistrate Wang Tung Li inquired about the
Dharma on Avalokiteśvara Mountain. At the invitation of upāsaka
Ho of Ch'iang's villa, I stayed a few days at that estate. I was also
provided with a boat which I took to pass Liang Ch'i and to visit
Hui Shan. Upāsaka Kao Ching I of the ministry of rites and others
invited me to a vegetarian dinner at the Chou clan's garden. Scholar
Wang, upāsaka Chang Chiu Fu and others of Lou Tung welcomed
me at the gate of the town; they came to pay reverence to me and
to hear the essentials of the Dharma. I then passed Wu Chiang and
met upāsakas Chou and Chen and others at the guest hall. Upāsaka
Yen Sheng awaited me at Sung Ling and invited me to his home.
They all followed me with vegetarian food and money for travelling expenses.

On the fifteenth day of the fourth month, I arrived at Chi Chao monastery. On the nineteenth, I performed the ceremony for the cremation of master Ta Kuan's body. His Buddhist and lay followers had already gathered there and I had written a funeral oration for the sacrificial services to him. The date I had anticipated tallied exactly with that of the ceremony. On the twenty-fifth, I personally collected the ashes which were placed in the Mañjuśrī tower. Then my disciple Fa K'ai erected a stūpa and I wrote the life story of the master which was to be engraved on the stūpa tablet; all this I did in fulfilment of my usual loyalty to my Dharma-friend. I stayed in the mountain to pass the new year and wrote *The Importance of Ch'an Practice* for the monks of the Ch'an hall. Fa K'ai inquired about the Dharmalakṣaṇa teaching and I wrote my book *The Interrelation Between the Noumenal and the Phenomenal*. For others who asked for instruction, I expounded Dharma-words to teach them and composed *The Song of the Fellow Carrying the Board*.

Upāsakas Chu Pai Min and Wang Chieh An of Wu Men called on me day and night and both of them tasted the joy of hearing the Dharma. At the time academician Ch'ien Shou Chih and secretary Yen Tien Chih of Yu Shan wrote inviting me to visit them. Magistrate Chin, chief Yu of the civil [administration] department, and the notables at Wu Lin sent welcoming letters. I could not accept their invitations as the end of the year was approaching.

Commentary by disciple Fu Cheng

The master's Foreword to his *Song of the Fellow Carrying the Board* reads as follows:

'In the Dharma Cave on Chin Shan Mountain since the time of Ch'an master Ta Hui who revived Lin Chi's doctrine, the Transmission was continued and each generation saw new achievements. However, now the Ch'an door has been desolate and silent for a long time. At present those who practise Ch'an are gathering on the mountain; some achieve stillness of mind in a flash of thought and thereby experience great comfort [when suddenly all feelings and passions vanish]. It is regrettable that

while sitting on the clean white ground [i.e. while realising this
state of cleanness] they consider it unique and refuse to forsake it,
not knowing that it will become a Dharma hindrance.[1] In the
Teaching School this is called the barrier of the known.[2] This is
why the ancient masters said: "You may reach the state of *Bright
Moon in the cold, deep pond* or that of the *Sound of the Bell in the
stillness of the night* without that state being disrupted by contact
with swelling water or rising waves and without deficiency even
in the midst of the loud beat and peal; but you are still on this
shore of birth and death." It is said: "It is easy to put one's feet on
a thorny bush, but it is difficult to turn one's body beneath the
bamboo screen in the bright moonlight." This is called "Holding
fast to the top of the pole with one's arm" or "the silent immers-
ion into stagnant water". Those who have reached the aforesaid
state are not allowed to abide there. How can one, who has not
even achieved it and has experienced the lightning flash of dhyāna
by chance, claim that he has achieved wisdom whereas he has
only trifled with the shadow of consciousness? This is a sickness
which is as common these days as it was in former times among
those who claim that they have attained when they are still incomplete. Apprehensive that those who have achieved this state
will fall into worldly ways and induce others into error, I compose *The Song of the Fellow Carrying the Board* for them after they
have asked for my instruction.'

The Song of the Fellow Carrying the Board

O Board bearer, O Board bearer! Why let it cheat you? You only
seek to lighten your shoulders but fail to look at the shackles
round your ankles. Even if you can bear it until you reach the
moment before birth,[3] half of that moment is already hidden by
it.

That board is like a cangue on your neck! It controls your

---

[1] Hindrance caused by attachment to dharma.
[2] The barrier of the known arises from regarding the seeming as the real.
[3] 'Moment before your birth' is the moment of the unperturbed mind.

whole body of flesh and bones. If you don't hurry to cast it off, it will become your real enemy for hundreds and thousands of aeons.

A shackle when you sit, a shackle when you walk! It's clearly a hindrance; why don't you recognise it? Only because from the start you have wrongly taken it for the real; a demon born in stillness.

You see it when your eyes are open; you see it when they are closed! It is like lightning in the clear sky in broad daylight. A mirage city which a simpleton takes for a deva palace.

If you want to lighten yourself, drop it down! What is the worth of a dead and fetid toad? Why do you replace the pupils of your eyes with black beans? Don't palm off fish eyes as real pearls.

There is a way, easy to tread! It is as easy and plain as a pair of scales. Just avoid hankering after attractive side-shows and in time you will enter the Imperial City.

Forsake body and life as you would the worthless earth! There is no need to avoid being reborn as a horse, a camel or a donkey.[1] If you can throw it beyond Mount Sumeru, even the hells of sword-leaf trees and hills of swords will be mere child's play for you.

If you love it, you will be ruined! Its hindrance is so recurrent that constant control is required. If you once break the crystal jug to pieces, the great earth, mountains and rivers will be pulverised.

Heed my advice: don't carry it! The skull dries up the moment it perspires.[2] Then there is continual parturition of the body and the projection of the image ad infinitum.[3] From then on, farewell to the gate of Death.[4]

[1] No need to avoid incarnation in the animal world which does not exist in the state of Bodhi.
[2] When the mind is reduced to the condition of a 'dry skull', well controlled and immutable, it automatically rejects all external influences.
[3] Buddha's power to reproduce himself ad infinitum and anywhere, in response to the needs of men.
[4] Farewell to continual incarnation in Saṁsāra.

My seventy-second year (1617–18)

On New Year's Day, I lectured on the Buddhist precepts.

I descended Shuang Ching Mountain and presented my condolence to the late master Yun Ch'i.[1] Over a thousand Buddhist and lay disciples had been waiting for me for some time on the mountain where I stayed for twenty days. Every evening we had a special meeting at which enquiries were made about the Dharma and which filled those who were present with great delight. I explained the esoteric practice followed by the late master Yun Ch'i during his lifetime. As his diciples heard this, some of them were moved to tears and said that I disclosed something that they had not known before. I was then invited to compose an inscription for the memorial stūpa.

When I left the mountain, Dharma-master Hsuan Ching and my follower T'an Neng Hsun along with the gentry and upāsakas of the district invited me to stay at the Tsung Ching hall of Chin Tzu monastery where, surrounded by a few thousand people, I lectured on the complete set of Mahāyāna Precepts. I wrote the story of Tsung Ching hall. At the time virtuous people from every side gathered on the lake and came with my follower T'an to inquire about the Dharma, each posing difficult questions. It was the greatest Dharma meeting which had ever taken place in the southeastern region. I then visited places noted for their scenery, such as Ling Yin, San Chu and Hsi Shan where I praised people setting fish free in the three ponds.[2] When I prepared to leave the government officials and upāsakas took boats to liberate fishes and gave a farewell dinner to us at the lake. They presented me with a petition inviting me to remain at Yun Ch'i monastery, where I agreed to stay for three years. I passed through Tsui Li [now Kashing in Chekiang province] where the chief of rites Yo Shih Fan and subprefect Hsiang Ch'u Tung, my two old friends, met me at Leng Yen monastery. As upāsaka Chen Lu Po of Lin Ch'i invited me to come

---

[1] Also called Lien Chih, a Ch'an master. There being few of high spirituality in his time, he urged his disciples to practise Pure Land teachings. His disciples did not even know he was an eminent Ch'an master.

[2] Where the fish were protected and people threw them cakes.

to his residence, I inquired during our conversation about the stūpa of my late master Yun Ku. He said: 'It's very near, just over a [Chinese] mile.' I was very glad and that evening I went to the temple where I paid reverence to my late master. The temple itself was a peaceful and beautiful place, but the stūpa was deserted and silent. I grieved for a long while and regretted that my hasty departure did not enable me to put the stūpa in order. I, therefore, requested upāsaka Chen to look after it for me and to acquire rice fields which would yield some income and ensure a regular supply of incense and lamp oil.

I entrusted Dharma-master Hsuan Ching and upāsaka T'an Meng Hsun with the compilation of records of my journeys and works in four books entitled *Journey to the East*. After my return to Wu Men, Dharma-masters Ch'ao Sung and I Yu invited me to go to Hua Shan Mountain. I visited places of scenic beauty such as Tien Chih, Hsuan Mu and T'ieh Shan. On Kuan Yin Mountain, upāsakas Chao Fan Fu, Wen Wen Chi, Yao Meng Chang, Hsu Chung Yung and Hsu Ch'ing Chih of Han Shan Mountain inquired about the Dharma. District magistrates Feng Yuan Cheng and Shen Hsuan Chu invited me to their homes; when I was about to leave [Wu Men], my disciples Tung Wen, Han Yueh, academician Ch'ien, Wang Chi H'u and Ch'u Wan Ch'u welcomed me to Ch'ang Shu. I went to Yu Shan where I passed two nights after which the academician of Fu Shui accompanied me to Ch'u A. Upāsaka Ho Chin Jen with his son and nephew awaited me in San Li monastery at Pen Nui and invited me to stay in the garden until the end of the summer retreat. I declined the invitation and returned to the mountain. He gave me a picture which I accepted of the Eighty-eight Patriarchs painted by a man of character named Ting Yun Peng. He then accompanied me to Ching K'ou where I was invited to a vegetarian dinner by the monks and lay Buddhists on San Shan Mountain. In the Ta Ch'e hall there, I gave lectures on the Buddhist precepts. After this I took a boat on my return trip to Kuang Shan.

On the first day of the fifth month, I passed Pai Hsia and spent the night on the river where I met one or two acquaintances. On the fifth day I arrived at Wu Hu. Officer Liu Yu Shou, who guarded the pass, invited me to stay and talk about remarkable dreams. Chief Ts'ui Ho Lou of the board of civil [administration] came and saw me on the river. On the sixteenth of the fifth month, the boat passed Hsing Chu and when I reached Kuei Tsung I stayed there. At the time subprefect Wang had already provided money for the erection of a vihāra for me. On the fifteenth of the sixth month, I ordered my disciple Fa Shan to supervise the construction at Wu Ju. The building was ready in the tenth month and I could thus dwell in peace.

Commentary by disciple Fu Cheng

I have witnessed about a hundred cases in which the master used his transcendental power; I will tell only a few important ones here:

(1) One day in Tsung Ching hall after the master had ascended the high seat, two monks supporting a third one came up the steps. The two implored the master to save their friend, saying: 'This mad monk has recited *The Avalokiteśvara Mantra* for five years and has never done anything wrong. We do not know why he is now tormented by a demon.' The master said: 'This can be cured.' He ordered his attendants to call in three persons who knew *The Mantra of the Vajra-Destroyer of Uncleanness*.[1] On the high seat the master recited the mantra first and ordered the three [who knew it] to teach the mad monk to recite it. At first the monk did not recover consciousness. The master knocked a stand with his fan making a sound and recited a sentence to teach the mad monk who then repeated it. The other three followed [this procedure] and recited the mantra sentence by sentence with the mad monk who was now able to recite it to the end. Then he awoke as from a dream, prostrated himself before the master and withdrew. The master ordered him to go to the kitchen hut where later he was found in good health. Those present that day included treasurer Wu Hsin K'o and others who did not believe

[1] *Mantras* are incantations. *Vajra-Destroyer* means indestructible destroyer. *Uncleanness* refers to karmic impurities caused by evil actions.

in transcendental power and were amazed after witnessing the incident.

(2) Another day a monk came, prostrated himself, and before he got up, the master knocked the stand with his fan and shouted: 'Murderer! Why do you come and see me!' The director of monastery affairs heard the shouting and came in a hurry. The monk kept silent and left. Those who were present were surprised and did not understand why the master had shouted. The following day it was reported that the monk had committed a robbery and been arrested. Incidents similar to the foregoing were many.

(3) On another occasion after a vegetarian meal, candles were lighted for tea and a special Ch'an meeting. The doors of the Ch'an hall were already closed. Suddenly a man holding a whip came and shouted outside. Those who knew him recognised him as Ch'ien Tsao Li of the tax office and thought that he was simply drunk. People tried to drive him away but he refused to leave, shouted louder and said, 'Today the living Bodhisattva has descended and I must be delivered. Why stop me?' I was very surprised when I heard this and reported it to the master who said: 'Bring him in.' When the man was admitted, he brought his palms together and saluted the master with the usual respect-inspiring deportment of a Buddhist monk. He knelt down and said: 'He is Ch'ien Ta Fu and I am Chung Yueh Jen. I am using his body as a medium to implore my deliverance. When I lived I was a vegetarian and practised the Pure Land teaching for eight years. Today is the fifth week after my death and if I am not sent to Hell, I ought to go to the Western Paradise. I hope the merciful Bodhisattva will show me the way and guide me.' After saying this he fell on his face and wept bitterly. My master ordered six old attendants who were well trained in the repetition of Amitābha Buddha's name, to stand up in the hall. The master held a string of beads and gave another one to the man. After the Buddha's name had been recited one thousand times, the medium could repeat it. After the repetition of the Buddha's name, the master expounded the text of the bestowal of food to hungry ghosts. When he came to the sentences:

'One should look into the Dharmadhātu;
All things are produced by mind alone . . .'

he beat the stand with his fan and shouted: 'Hasten your deliverance!' The man did likewise and said: 'Delivered!' The master shouted three times and the man repeated three times, more quickly than an echo. Then the man got up and with his respect-inspiring deportment thanked the master for ferrying him to the Pure Land. He turned to the right and left and saluted those present, saying: 'Please do your utmost. I will meet you all at the Dragon-Flower-Tree assembly.'[1] More than a night watch elapsed and the hall was crowded with people, some being moved to tears, some praising the master, some secretly laughing at him and some even criticising him. The master remained unmoved and took a sedan chair to return to the boat. The man followed the chair and accompanied the master to the river bank where he prostrated himself again to thank him. Then he returned to the entrance of the Ch'an hall where he thanked Ch'ien Tsao Li for loaning his physical body as a medium and so enabling him to be ferried to the other shore. Then he fell down and when he awoke, it was the same tax collector Ch'ien Tsao Li with his usual deportment.

In the hall someone said that Chung Yueh Jen was the father of a scholar who lived on the opposite side of the river and was well known at Shao Chou. The father was an earnest devotee of the Pure Land school, thus explaining the prompt response to his appeal for deliverance. I said: 'This scholar is Chung Sheng Fu, a member of our Buddhist group.' I then took a few friends with me and called on Chung Sheng Fu whom I took to the boat to see the master. I learned from him that it was exactly the fifth week after the death of his father. Tax collector Ch'ien Tsao Li had gone that day to Chung's house to collect the tax. Because he

---

[1] *The Dragon-Flower-Tree* will be the Bodhi tree of Maitreya, the Buddhist Messiah when he comes to earth. Maitreya will be the next Buddha; he is now in the Tusiṭa heaven and is expected to come five thousand years after Śākyamuni Buddha.

was drunk when he stood before the funeral tablet, his body was seized and used as a medium for the purpose here described.

My seventy-third year (1618–19)
Upāsaka Wu and others gave donations for the erection of a vihāra for me in which to pass my old age. The Buddha shrine and Ch'an hall at Wu Ju were repaired only that year. In the third month councillor Ch'en Ch'ih Shih of Fou Liang came to the mountain; and with Pao Chung Su of the bureau of rites at Hsin An and Hsia Wo Ch'i of the bureau of punishment at Hsing Tzu, he formed a group of ten friends to provide funds for these repairs which were completed in the fifth month.

My seventy-fourth year (1619–20)
That spring in the first month, I recited *The Avataṁsaka Sūtra* which took a long time. I explained my *Commentary on The Lotus Sūtra*. In that summer I gave talks on *The Śūraṅgama Sūtra*, *The Awakening of Faith*, *The Diamond Sūtra*, *The Sūtra of Complete Enlightenment* and *The Vijñaptimātrasiddhi Śāstra*. In the seventh month of that autumn, I requested prefect Yuan of Nan K'ang to record the decision that Wu Ju was to become a permanent home for old monks coming from all quarters.

On the fifteenth day of the eighth month, I did not receive visitors and isolated myself for meditation. I followed the example set by Dharma-master Hui Yuan and used incense sticks for measuring time to practise concentration according to the Pure Land school.

I thought of the Avataṁsaka school which was about to be discontinued and of Dharma-master Ch'ing Liang's commentary which was found to be too extensive and cumbersome by all those who had read it, could not grasp its meaning and thus put it aside. As Ch'ing Liang was our country's first commentator on that sūtra, my belief was that if he were dropped the school also would be discontinued. For this reason I intended to use his commentary and to condense it in order to get a general idea of the sūtra and enable readers to understand it. I gave the condensed commentary the title of *The Essentials of The Avataṁsaka Sūtra*. During my retreat, I began to read it and started my work.

My seventy-fifth year (1620–1)
In the spring when my meditation was over, my attendant Kuang I asked me to explain *The Sūtra of Complete Enlightenment*, *The Awakening of Faith* and *The Seven Chapters of Chuang Tzu Metaphysics*.

That summer I suffered from pains in my feet. That autumn in the eighth month, the official of rites Ch'en Wu I of Ma Ch'eng, chief Hsu Ming Heng of the rites office at An I, chief Wu Hsun Shang of the criminal department at Hsing Tzu, envoy Lu Ching Yeh of Chiang Chou, prefect Yuan Chiu Chi of Nan K'ang and judge Li Chung Ta came to the mountain to enquire about the Dharma. Provincial inspector Wu of Hu Nan who had been transferred to the post of chief justice of Kuang Tung went to Ts'ao Ch'i to pay reverence to the Sixth Patriarch and requested my disciples there to ask me to write the life stories of the Patriarchs. In my illness I wrote seventy stories, each with an eulogy and in my own hand. Eight years had now passed since I left Ts'ao Ch'i to come to Nan Yo and stay on Kuang Shan Mountain. All the monks at Ts'ao Ch'i had invited me to return there several times without result. On his way to his post, inspector Wu went to the mountain where he saw the monastery that I had rebuilt. He praised my work and was informed by the monks of their desire and failure to have me return there. Inspector Wu gladly promised to be the protector of the Dharma and wrote to invite me. The whole monastery and the gentry of the district also sent their joint invitation. My Cantonese disciple, censor Wang Sheng Tung, came personally with the letters three times to Kuang Shan Mountain, but I declined their invitations on the grounds of illness.

My seventy-sixth year (1621–2)
In the summer complying with my followers' request, I explained my *Commentary on The Laṅkāvatāra Sūtra*. In the tenth month of that winter, scholar Liu Chi Hsiang, Ch'en Ti Hsiang, Ch'en Ti Shun

and Liang Szu Hsiang, who were my disciples, wrote to me requesting my return to Ts'ao Ch'i. At the same time, ex-intendant Chu
of Shao Yang circuit, who had been transferred to the maritime
inspectorate, and justice Wu came again to Kuang Shan Mountain
with letters inviting me to Ts'ao Ch'i, but again I declined because
of illness.

My seventy-seventh year (1622–3)
I continued my work on *The Essentials of The Avataṁsaka Sūtra* and
completed it. My followers asked me to lecture on *The Śūraṅgama
Sūtra, The Sūtra of Complete Enlightenment, The Awakening of Faith*
and *Chao Lun.* Provincial justice Wu returned from an audience
with the emperor and wrote again expressing his earnest desire to
invite me back to Ts'ao Ch'i. Prefect Chang San Hsing of Shao
Yang sent me a special letter which was brought by bhikṣu Pen Ang,
head of the monastery's hall. As it was no longer possible to decline
their invitations, I decided to go to Ts'ao Ch'i once more. On the
tenth day of the eleventh month, I left Kuang Shan Mountain and
crossed P'eng Hu Lake, writing a poem on the occasion. Soon
administrator Chou Nan Kao who was on his way to the North
went to Kuang Shan to see me but missed me as I was already at Chi
Chou where I met Hsiao Chueh Hsiu who was an academician, Ma
Chi Fang, Ts'ang Yao Ch'en, Liu Shao Yeh, Ho K'e Shang and Liu
Chuan Hua. These gentlemen inquired about the Dharma at Tzu
Yen hall on the mountain.

On the eighth day of the twelfth month, I crossed Ta Yu Peak
and on the fifteenth day I arrived at Ts'ao Ch'i.

(Master Han Shan's Autobiography ends here)

The master's seventy-eighth year (1623–4)
The master stayed in the Ch'an hall at Ts'ao Ch'i. Prefect Chang of
Shao Yang and the nobility and gentry of the prefecture went to
the mountain to invite him to expound the Dharma.

That spring in the third month, the master's disciples from Fa
Hsin monastery at Wu Yang arrived. He taught them the complete

Buddhist precepts and then lectured on *The Awakening of Faith*, *The Vijñaptimātrasiddhi Śāstra* and *The Śūraṅgama Sūtra*.

In the fifth month of that summer, scholars Ma Chi Fang and Wang Tei Tsou of Chi Chou called on the master.

In the eighth month of that autumn, after receiving visitors, the master sent his attendant to offer his thanks to treasurer Wu. As the attendant was about to leave, the master said: 'When the Buddhas and Patriarchs proclaimed the Truth widely in order to convert the people, its worthiness depended on the propitiousness of both time and cause. No good result can be expected if the time and cause are not suitable. A lifetime's work being over, I am going back. . . .' Those who were present were at a loss to understand him and thought he was talking about returning to Kuang Shan Mountain. The master composed a poem entitled 'Mid-autumn without Moonlight'.[1]

After the ninth day of the ninth month, the master wrote for his attendant Shen Kuang a foreword to a poem entitled 'The Stay on the Mountain'. It read: 'Although this old man is slothful in using the writing brush and inkstone, he is apprehensive that once his breath does not return there will be a liability in the next life. If this is looked upon as a simple poem, great injustice, indeed, will be done to him [master Han Shan].'

On the first of the tenth month, his disciple Tung Chiung arrived from Kuang Shan Mountain. The master asked about the monks there and about his old friends at the other monasteries in that region, and was very happy at hearing news of them. At the time his disciple Chin Tai asked him to write an outline of his life's work. On the third day district magistrate Hsiao Hsuan P'u came to the mountain to see the master and they had a long chat that lasted three days and nights. They were delighted. When Hsiao asked about the essentials of the Dharma, the master wrote two compositions of Dharma-words and three poems for him. On the sixth day when Hsiao left the mountain, the master told him: 'The population of this region put all their confidence in you. Take good care of your-

[1] Usually the moon is never as round and bright as in mid-autumn. The poem foretold his death.

self.' The magistrate, wanting to see him again, asked for a date. The master said: 'The monk of the mountain is already old, and the four elements will scatter very soon. I will meet you at the Dragon Flower Assembly.'

On the eighth day, the master showed some slight symptoms of indisposition; when his disciples asked about his health, he merely said: 'The old man is tired but not ill.' On the ninth day, when medicine was brought he refused it, saying: 'I am leaving. What is the use of taking medicine?' Hearing this, his disciple Kuang I was frightened and asked: 'If you are really leaving, what instruction will you leave us?' The master scolded him and said: 'You have been my attendant for so long; how can you still hold such a view? You should remember that the question of birth and death is important and that impermanence never rests for a moment. Think earnestly of the Buddha.' Kuang said: 'If you don't give us a single word as instruction, what shall we observe for our guidance?' The master replied: 'Even the proclamations of the Golden Mouth [Buddha's mouth] have become old paper. My words will certainly become useless.' Consequently, he did not utter a single word.

On the twelfth, which was the master's birthday, his Buddhist and lay disciples gathered in the monastery. Prefect Chang San Hsing of Shao Yang came to the mountain and presented him with a thin purple robe as a birthday gift. He and the master chatted all day and at sunset the prefect withdrew. That evening the master took a bath and the next morning wore the new robe that he had received from the prefect. As the latter approached the bed, the master said: 'The monk of the mountain is leaving. . . . Many thanks for your protection of the Dharma.' Prefect Chang consoled him and said: 'Master, you are not ill. I am the guardian of this region and, therefore, the host; I will assume full responsibility.' The master smiled, closed the palms of his hands and again thanked his visitor. At noon the prefect departed. The master ordered his attendant to bring him fresh water to rinse his mouth. He said: 'Today all creepers[1] will be cut off.' Then he ordered a bath and changed his garments. All those present stood round him to repeat the Buddha's

[1] Worthless worldly connections.

name. He said: 'Do not be frightened but act according to Buddhist
custom: no mourning and no weeping, but repetition of the
Buddha's name with a single mind.' At the Shen hour,[1] he passed
away while sitting upright. That evening the sky was lit by radiant
rays, flocks of birds cried mournfully while monks and laymen
were broken-hearted and their cries shook the mountain and the
valley.

Three days after the master's death, his face was still radiant and
his lips red; his hands and feet were still pliable as if he were in the
state of Samādhi. The sad news was reported to prefect Chang who
sent officials to present condolences.

When the body was placed in a coffin, it was only five days after
magistrate Hsiao had left the mountain and was still at Hsiung Chou
where he received the sad tidings. At first he was sorrowful for the
whole day; but when he received the more detailed information
about the circumstances preceding the master's death, his face
beamed with delight and he said: 'The master was one of those in
the rank of the holy. If he had not seen through the crisis of birth
and death, how could he have done so at the last moment?' He wrote
a composition for a pair of scrolls to comfort the master and gave a
donation of one hundred taels. He also wrote to the prefects of the
two Nan Shao districts requesting them to build an image hall for
worshipping the master.

Upon hearing the news of the master's death, his followers on
Wu Ju Peak of Kuan Shan Mountain, Fu Shan among others, came
to Ts'ao Ch'i to execute his will by taking the coffin to Wu Ju where
they erected a stūpa at a site previously selected by the master himself. At the same time the image hall was completed. [Bhikṣus] Ku
Liu, Fu Shan and others contacted academician Wu, magistrate
Wu, treasurer Sheng, officials Wang Man Su and Miu Mu T'ai,
requesting them to petition the authorities with a view to fulfilling
the necessary formalities for taking the coffin to Kuang Shan
Mountain. . . . It left the monastery [at Ts'ao Ch'i] on the twenty-
first day of the first month of the fifth year of the reign of T'ien
Chi [February 1625] and arrived at Fa Yun monastery of Wu Ju

[1] From 3 to 5 p.m.

Peak at Kuang Shan Mountain on the twenty-eighth day of the second month [April 1625].

Commentary by disciple Fu Cheng

On the twenty-first day of the first month of the fifth year of the T'ien Chi reign [February 1625], the coffin was taken to Kuang Shan Mountain. Because of the wet and shady ground there, [Bhikṣu] Fu Shan erected a stūpa hall in which the coffin was placed for worship. Prefect Ch'ien Wu Hsin of Nan K'ang selected a site where the coffin was buried. Eleven years elapsed and in the year I Hai (1635–6) the mountain was infested with tigers. Disquiet reigned in the monastery and [Bhikṣu] Fu Shan attributed all this to the burying ground being unsuitable. Consequently, the coffin was disinterred and placed again in the stūpa for worship. It was discovered that half of it had been eaten by white ants and no one dared to bury it again. Another nine years passed and in the ninth month of the year Kuei Wei (1643), the minister of rites Ch'en Tzu Chuang of Ling Nan, who was the master's disciple, sent a letter with funds [to Kuang Shan Mountain) to welcome the coffin back to Ts'ao Ch'i. It happened that at the same time, another disciple, Liu Chi Hsiang, who was head of the board of punishment at Jui Chou and was making an investigation at Nan K'ang, took charge of the delivery and transportation of the coffin to Ts'ao Ch'i. When the convoy reached Mei Ling, the master's Dharma-friend Sung Chao Ming, the newly appointed defence commissioner of Kuang Tung, was passing the Ta Yu Peak and met the procession there. Overcome with joy at the fortunate coincidence, he ordered his soldiers to carry the coffin which he personally accompanied to Ts'ao Ch'i. A few months later after he had taken up his new post, he went to Ts'ao Ch'i again. When bhikṣus Kuang Cheng and Tzu Li were carrying the coffin they had noticed it had cracked. Through one of the cracks, they could see the body, as if the master was alive, in a sitting position. They talked about opening the coffin but no one dared to make a decision. Commissioner Sung heard of their deliberation and, with his sword pierced through one of the cracks and split the coffin open. The body was seated with crossed legs as if the master were alive; his hair and nails had grown long; his complexion was bright red and his garments, although they looked new, fell to pieces exposing the naked body when they were fully exposed to the air. Suddenly a monk came and requested that the Indian custom be followed of plastering the body with sandalwood dust as if varnished with lacquer. When this was done, the monk departed.

When the master was staying at Ts'ao Ch'i, a virgin took a vow to make him an embroidered one thousand Buddhas robe. She was afraid that her breath was not pure and masked her mouth with a piece of yellow silk while she was making it. When her work was completed, the master had passed away and his body had already been placed in the coffin. The robe was, therefore, left at Ts'ao Ch'i monastery. When the coffin was returned to Ts'ao Ch'i and opened, the master's garments fell to pieces, which the villagers gathered and kept for good luck. The robe made by the virgin was still like new in spite of the fact that some twenty-two years had elapsed; it was taken out of the monastery's storehouse and put on the master's body which was placed in the stūpa hall, now named Han Shan's temple and located about half a [Chinese] mile from the Sixth Patriarch's monastery. Every morning at day break, a vessel of hot incense water was used to perfume the master's face which perspired and was dried with a towel. Vegetarian food was offered just as if he were alive. Once every year the body was bathed, and the villagers kept the holy water and drank it whenever they became ill.

GLOSSARY

Āgamas: A collection of Hīnayāna doctrines. The Four *Āgamas* are: Dīrghāgama, or 'Long' treatises, Madhyamāgama, or 'Middle' treatises, Saṁyuktāgama, or 'Miscellaneous' treatises and Ekottarāgama or 'Numerical' treatises.

Asaṅkhyeyas: Countless aeons.

Avalokiteśvara: Goddess of Mercy in China, so called because of his appearing as a benevolent lady. He attained enlightenment by means of the faculty of hearing. (See *The Śūraṅgama Sūtra.* Rider, London.)

Avataṁsaka Sūtra: The first long sūtra expounded by the Buddha after His Enlightenment.

Awakening of Faith: Its Sanskrit title is 'Śraddhotpāda-śāstra' and its full Chinese title is 'Awakening of Faith of Mahāyāna school'. It is attributed to Aśvaghoṣa and gives the fundamental principles of Mahāyāna.

Awakening, Spiritual: Chinese, *wu,* and Japanese, *satori;* a state in which a disciple is free from thinking and discrimination to enter into the region of reality; usually he passes through several minor and major stages of awakening before attaining complete Enlightenment.

Bhūtatathatā: Bhūta is substance, that which exists; tathatā is suchness, thusness, i.e. such is its nature. It means the real, thus always, or eternally so; i.e. reality as contrasted with unreality, or appearance, and the unchanging or immutable as contrasted with form and phenomena.

Bodhi: Enlightenment.

Buddha: The Enlightened One; the first of the Triple Gem, the second being Dharma and the third, Saṅgha.

Ch'an: Name of mind; Ch'an being name and mind being substance; wrongly interpreted as meditation, abstraction, or dhyāna in Sanskrit (Jap., Zen).

Chao Lun: A treatise written in the fourth century by Seng Chao, a disciple of Kumārajīva.

Chih Kuan: See T'ien T'ai School.

Dāna-pāramitā: See Six Pāramitās.

Deva: The gods, the highest incarnations of the six worlds of existence.

Dharma: Law, truth, religion, thing, anything Buddhist. It connotes Buddhism as the perfect religion; it has the second place in the Triratna or Triple Gem.

Dharma-dhātu: The unifying and underlying spiritual reality that is regarded as the ground or cause of all things; the absolute from which all things proceed.

Dharmakāya: Body in its essential nature, or that of Buddha as such; it is visible to Buddhas only.

Dharmalakṣaṇa: Aspects and characteristics of things.

Dharmatā: The underlying nature of all things.

Dhyāna: Stillness of mind; serenity.

Dhyāna-pāramitā: See Six Pāramitās.

Diamond Sūtra: Its Sanskrit title is *Vajracchedikā-prajñā-pāramitā-sūtra*. Cf *Ch'an and Zen Teaching, First Series,* part III, pp. 147–206, A Commentary on The Diamond Sūtra by Ch'an master Han Shan. Rider, London.

Eightfold Correct Path: Aṣṭa-mārga—correct view, correct thought, correct speech, correct conduct, correct livelihood, correct devotion, correct mindfulness and correct meditation.

Four Noble Truths: Catvāriārya-satyāni, the four dogmas which are: suffering (duḥkha), its cause (samudāya), its ending (nirodha) and the way thereto (mārga). They are the doctrines first preached by the Buddha to His five former ascetic companions, and those who accepted them were in the śrāvaka stage.

Gāthā: Poems or chants; one of the twelve divisions of the Mahāyāna canon.

Guru: A spiritual master; a preceptor who guides his students to the other shore of Enlightenment.

Heart Sūtra: Its full title is Prajñā-Pāramitā-Hṛdaya-sūtra. Cf *Ch'an and Zen Teaching, First Series,* part IV, *A Straight Talk on the Heart Sūtra,* by Ch'an master Han Shan. Rider, London.

Hīnayāna: 'Small Vehicle', also called 'Half-word', preliminary teaching given by the Buddha to His disciples who were still not qualified for receiving His Mahāyāna doctrines, called 'Whole-word'. It is based on the three signata or three Dharma seals of impermanence, egolessness and peace in nirvāṇa.

Hīnayāna attainment, The four stages of: Śrota-āpanna, entering the holy stream; Sakṛdāgāmin, once more to come or be reborn in the world of desire; anāgāmin, no coming or no more rebirth; and arhatship, beyond the worldly way.

Kalpa: Aeon; period of time too long to be measured.

Karma: Moral action causing future retribution, and either good or evil transmigration.

Karmadāna: Duty distributor, second in command in a monastery.

Kleśa: Worry, anxiety, trouble, distress and whatever causes them.

Kṣamayati: Confession and asking for pardon.

Kṣanti-pāramitā: See Six Pāramitās.

Kung An: Japanese, Koan; dossier, case-record, public laws and regulations enforced for settling disputes and maintaining law and order. Likewise all instructions given by enlightened masters to their students are called kung ans, or concurrent causes. The meaning of a kung an is irrevocable for it is as valid as the law.

Lin Chi: Master I Hsuan of Lin Chi (Jap., Rinzai), disciple of Huang Po and founder of the Lin Chi sect, one of the five Ch'an sects of China. Died in 867.

Lotus Sūtra: Its full title is *Saddharma-puṇḍarīka-sūtra.* It was expounded during the last years of the Buddha's life to teach the one Buddha vehicle which transcends the three expedient vehicles of śrāvakas, pratyeka-buddhas and Bodhisattvas.

Mahāmudrā: Tibet Yoga of Great Symbol which teaches pointed concentration for mystic insight into the underlying nature of all things and attainment of nirvāṇa.

Mahāparinirvāṇa-sūtra: The last sūtra expounded by the Buddha in a day and night to reveal the four absolute realities of eternity, bliss, self or entity and purity in the ultimate nirvāṇa in contrast with impermanence, pleasure, ego and filthiness in saṁsāra.

Mahāyāna: The Great Vehicle which indicates Universalism, or Salvation for all, for all are Buddhas and will attain Enlightenment. It teaches the six perfections or pāramitās. (See Six Pāramitās.)

Mokṣa Pariṣad: A great assembly for the confession of sins, the inculcation of morality and discipline, and the distribution of charity.

Nirmānakāya: Transformed body of a Buddha, that of power to transform himself at will into any form for the omnipresent salvation of those needing him. It is perceptible to men.

Nirvāṇa: Complete extinction of individual existence; cessation of rebirth and entry into bliss.

Prajñā: Transcendental wisdom.

Prajñā-pāramitā: See Six Pāramitās.

Prajñā sūtras: The wisdom sūtras, especially *the Mahāprajñā-pāramitā-sūtra*, said to have been explained by the Buddha in four places at sixteen assemblies. It consists of 600 chuans or rolls bound in 120 volumes, as translated by Hsuan Tsang and is the fundamental work of the Mahāyāna school on wisdom, which is the sixth pāramitā.

Pratyeka-buddha: One who lives apart from others and attains Enlightenment alone, or for himself, in contrast with the altruism of the Bodhisattva principle.

Pure Land school: A Buddhist sect which teaches intense concentration on Amitābha Buddha by calling His name and by meditating on Him and His two attendant Bodhisattvas, Avalokiteśvara and Mahāsthāma, that is the three Holy Ones in the Western Paradise of Bliss, for one's rebirth there in order to receive their teaching of the Dharma thereby realising supreme Enlightenment.

Samādhi: State of mental imperturbability, free from all external sensation.

Samādhibala: The power of samādhi to overcome all disturbing thoughts, including fear.

Samādhi of the ocean symbol: The vastness of meditation which reveals all phenomena as springing from the underlying reality.

Samantabhadra: A Bodhisattva, symbol of the fundamental law, dhyāna and the practice of all Buddhas. He is the right-hand assistant of the Buddha, and Mañjuśrī is his left-hand assistant. His region is in the East. Mount O Mei in Szechwan, China, is his bodhimaṇḍala or holy site, and devotees go there to see myriad Buddha lamps in the sky at night.

Śamatha-vipaśyanā: See T'ien T'ai School.

Sambhoga-kāya: Reward body of a Buddha, that of bliss and enjoyment of the fruits of his past saving labours. It is visible to Bodhisattvas.

Saṅgha: The Buddhist order, the last of the Triple Gem.

Śīla-pāramitā: See Six Pāramitās.

Six Pāramitās: Translated as 'six perfections' in the West, or six methods of attaining Enlightenment: dāna (charity), śīla (discipline), kṣanti (patience or endurance), vīrya (zeal and progress), dhyāna (meditation or serenity) and prajñā (wisdom).

Śrāvaka: A hearer, disciple of the Buddha who understands the Four Noble Truths, rids himself of the unreality of the phenomenal and enters the incomplete nirvāṇa.

Śūraṅgama sūtra: Leng Yen Ching, a sūtra translated by Pāramiti in 705, in which the Buddha revealed the causes of illusion leading to the creation of all worlds of existence and the method of getting out of them. Rider, London.

Sūtra of Complete Enlightenment: Cf *Ch'an and Zen Teaching, Third Series,* part III, pp. 147–278. *Rider, London*

T'ien T'ai school: A Buddhist sect which teaches *chih* or silencing the active mind to stop all thinking and discrimination, and *kuan* or looking into the mind thus disengaged from them to restore our inherent Buddha-nature. Chih and Kuan are śamatha and vipaśyanā in Sanskrit.

Tripiṭaka: The Buddhist canon consisting of three divisions: sūtras (sermons), vinaya (rules of morality and discipline) and śāstras (treatises).

Twelve links in the chain of existence: The twelve nidānas: avidyā, unenlightenment; saṁskāra, disposition; vijñāna, consciousness; nāmarūpa, name and form; ṣaḍāyatana, the six sense organs; sparśa, touch; vedanā, sensation; tṛṣṇā, desire; upādāna, grasping; bhāva, becoming; jāti, birth; jarāmaraṇa, old age and death.

Ullambana: Festival of All Souls which is held on the fifteenth day of the seventh month; sūtras are read and offerings made to the Buddhist Trinity for the release from purgatory of the spirits of those who have died on land or sea.

Upāsaka: A male lay disciple who engages to observe the first five rules of morality.

Upāsikā: A female lay disciple who engages to observe the first five rules of morality.

Vaipulya: Expanded sūtras; one of the twelve divisions of the Mahāyāna canon.

Vairocana: The chief of the five Dhyāni Buddhas, occupying the central position. Vairocana is called the Great Sun Tathāgata and is generally recognised as the spiritual or essential body of Buddha-truth, and like light pervading everywhere. According to the T'ien T'ai school, Vairocana represents the Dharmakāya, Rocana or Locana the Sambhogakāya and Śākyamuni the Nirmāṇakāya.

Vajradhātu: The realm of the indestructive diamond-brilliant mind, the spiritual world of complete Enlightenment.

Vijñapti-mātra-siddhi-śāstra: A treatise of the Dharmalakṣaṇa school which holds that all is mind in its ultimate nature.

Virya-pāramitā: See Six Pāramitās.